SS HANDBLÄTTER
FÜR DEN WELTANSCHAULICHEN UNTERRICHT

Handbills for the Worldview education of the troops

Translator: S. Kerr B.A. (Hons)

First published 2022 by Realhistorybooks.co.uk

INTRODUCTION

It has taken almost 18 years of research and numerous visits to Europe to be able to find a complete set of these handbills in their original wallet. These were not mass produced as they were only issued to officers responsible for the ideological training of the Waffen ⚡⚡ troops.

They were produced on paper and issued in a simple card wallet so not designed for longevity. Then the harsh conditions imposed by the Allies and the introduction of the "De-Nazification process" and the unprecedented designation and outlawing of a section of a nations armed forces as a "Criminal Organisation" made mere possession of this document literally a hanging offence.

In such circumstances not many of these wallets survive. Individual handbills have appeared, but no-one has ever been able to present the complete collection which you now hold in your hands.

The book that you hold now is considered controversial by some. Others may even believe that it should never have been published due to the language it uses in parts.

However, knowledge cannot, and should not, be censored. The events of WW2, as with many earlier events, have shaped the world in which we live today, therefore we must learn from the past. We do not seek to promote nor condemn the contents of this book, that is in the remit of the reader alone. No organised group, publisher or book seller, such as Amazon, should be able to dictate what is and is not suitable reading material. The last few years have seen thousands of books removed from sale or withdrawn from public libraries because one special interest group or another feels "offended" and does not want you to make a judgement for yourself as to the contents of such books.

It has long been a mystery for historians as to why hundreds of thousands of young European men would join the Waffen-⚡⚡. This book, at least in part, provides that answer.

TABLE OF CONTENTS

25 Topics for the handbills

Introductory notes for the lecturer

There is no single method of teaching.

I. The teaching method is determined by a number of factors;

1. It depends on the person of the teacher, who naturally imposes a personal touch on his teaching. The natural born speaker will proceed differently from the non-speaker, but this does not mean that the non-speaker cannot achieve the same success in his education as the speaker;

2. It must depend on the level of education of the ϟϟ-men, and

3. It depends on the subject matter itself.

The success of teaching depends ultimately not on methods, on rules and laws, but on the personality which instructs and forms the ϟϟ-man.

In each case, the best method is the one that turns men into fanatical National Socialist fighters.

II. Teaching methods are lecture and discussion

They both have their merits. But it is impossible to reach the desired goal only by lecture or only by instructional discussion.

An example of this: The unit leader who addresses his listeners only with lectures will soon find that his men, even if they were greatly impressed by his lectures, have not mastered the subject matter. And once the subject matter is forgotten, the ideological insights and the driving forces aroused by the lecture are also lost.

Conversely, the teaching talk cannot be used everywhere exclusively. For example, it is not possible to start a lecture if the subject matter to be taught is completely unknown, because a lecture pre-supposes a certain amount of knowledge of the subject matter.

III. The Lecture

The unit leader is always forced to present his material to the men in the form of a lecture if the material is completely new. If, for example, the subject matter in history is from the past, then the lecture is to be given preference; it must then help the historical lesson to its true dignity. It is best to give a free lecture, because it then achieves the best effect. A prerequisite for every lecture is good preparation. The listener must not only be able to hear the historical events in the lecture, but also a passionate inner sympathy on the part of the speaker.

It is also important that the men's gaze is directed to maps and pictures during the lecture, which promotes understanding, keeps the listeners in suspense and helps them to fight fatigue.

The lecture should always be followed by a discussion in which the subject matter is clarified, anchored in the memory and examined and evaluated in terms of its ideological insights.

IV. The teaching talk

The teaching talk presupposes a certain knowledge of the subject matter. This does not mean that every ⚡⚡-man must be able to tell the subject matter at the drop of a hat and be able to reproduce the thought content. What is meant is that it is possible to raise the awareness of the men to be trained of the ideas that belong to the common elaboration of a topic from the entire field of knowledge and experience. Where gaps in knowledge occur, the material is supplemented by the unit leader himself.

Let us think of heredity, for example. It would be unwise for the unit leader to start with a big lecture. He only has to ask the men to tell where and when they have observed signs of heredity in humans, animals and plants, and soon the teaching discussion is underway. Once the first has given an example, the second will soon follow. One is encouraged to cooperate by the other.

Such a discussion has great advantages. Everyone feels addressed, everyone can contribute their knowledge and experience. Without wanting to, the man is encouraged to participate by the liveliness of the community.

Some dare to come out with questions and answers, practise speaking in front of a crowd of men, which they would otherwise hardly ever attempt.

One enriches the other with his knowledge, and all bring home the fruits that the communal work has allowed to ripen.

The doctrinal conversation exercises the men's speaking, thinking and judgement and is a good preparation for the case that the man has to deal with doubters and naysayers.

Often questions and answers are a back and forth between unit leader and men. In some cases, the answer complements the question with only one word. This form, while not entirely avoidable, is far from the best. One should therefore avoid, if possible, asking questions whose answer only requires individual pieces to be incorporated into the question asked. It is better to throw a small problem into the audience. Then everyone must try to take a position on this problem. The first person takes up the problem by giving his opinion, another adds to the first answer, a third perhaps takes a stand on the problem from another side of the consideration, a fourth challenges the correctness, and a fifth finally creates final clarity. Each person can contribute to the solution of the problem through his or her knowledge and judgement. Through this form of instructional discussion, the unit leader creates a constant "state of alert", which encourages everyone to participate in the joint, humane working out of the material, and which educates for independent thinking, judgement and the free exchange of opinions.

What is the role of the teacher in such a discussion?

He is apparently quite passive, but only apparently. The teacher must have a precise idea of the course of the discussion as early as the preparatory stage. He must also be completely aware of the teaching material. He makes sure that the discussion does not get out of hand. He also makes sure that the discussion is not conducted only by those who have the greater knowledge. He must sometimes impose restrictions and restraints on those who are spiritually strong, but encourage those who are spiritually weak. Wherever one has deviated from the line of thought or wants to lapse into a discussion, the unit leader must stop immediately and steer the conversation back on the right track. Alternately, he throws questions, observation tasks, small problems, suggestions and additions into the circle of listeners, which are taken up and worked on by the listeners.

At the end of the lecture, the leader summarises the material covered, and the lessons learned for the life of the ϟϟ-man according to a disposition worked out by the community.

The teaching talk demands the strongest concentration from the leader. Here it becomes clear whether he is really the spiritual and ideological leader of his men. One should not believe that the first teaching talk will take place immediately as described here. It requires a lot of practice and some self-conquest, until the leader is completely unbiased in every situation and until his listeners have grown together into a real working community. But once he has accustomed his men to these instructional discussions, all inhibitions on both sides are removed, and the unit leader has the best methodical means in his hand for "*planned training instruction*", for "*practical instruction*" and for discussing the "*events of the day and the political situation*".

V. The visual aids

1. The map

No matter how effective the spoken word may be, it will be better received and better understood if the guidance of thought is also supported by the eye. The unit leader must make it a rule to let every new piece of material reach consciousness through as many senses as possible; for the senses are the gates of the soul through which man absorbs the things and processes of reality.

It is therefore self-evident that in every history lesson the map is present; without a map one cannot teach history. History lessons also offer numerous opportunities to compensate for the deficiencies of the men's knowledge of geography with the help of the map.

The numerous maps in the material collections clearly indicate the importance attached to illustration by means of the map.

2 The picture

If possible, pictures should also be used in teaching, as they speak an even clearer language than maps. Of course, the picture strip is one of these visual aids. Subjects of racial studies and racial politics cannot be taught at all without pictures.

The value of the picture for teaching is also considered in the subject matter collections.

3 Film

Film is the most modern means of illustration. The importance it will one day acquire for teaching cannot yet be overlooked.

Here, in a few words, we will look at the characteristics of film. The picture captures a state, the film, on the other hand, draws its content from the realm of the moving and living. Image and film are related to each other like static and dynamic.

What is the reason for the strong attraction of film?

a) It is the best understood of all images and needs little or no explanation from the standard guide, like maps and images.

b) The movement of the pictures strongly attracts the attention of men.

c) The film comes closest to the real course of events in life.

Apart from the book of reality, no book is better to read than the picture book of film.

d) The film is not restricted in any way. It rules over space and time. Thus, film has become a great power in all fields of communication.

If a film can be used for training and education in the ⚡⚡, it must be used without fail ("*The Great King*", "*Bismarck*", "*The Dismissal*", etc.

VI. The course of a lesson

A. Preparation for the lesson

Each lesson requires thorough preparation by the unit leader.

This preparation includes:

1. The formulation of a clear teaching objective (heading). See the examples on the lesson sheets! The aim of the lesson must be formulated in such a way that all the ideas of the ⚡⚡-men which are in contact with the new subject matter are immediately brought to life and the ⚡⚡-man listens with interest.

If no such related ideas are dormant in the listeners' minds, the unit leader must create an inner relationship to the new material through introductory questions or explanations.

2. A precise delimitation of the material to be studied and evaluated in one lesson.

3. To define the material, i.e., to find a form of expression for the lecture or discussion, which is suitable for the men's comprehension.

4. To check which visual aids can be used (map, picture, picture strip).

5. Deciding whether the material should be taught by lecture or by discussion. If the lecture is the first step, a subsequent discussion is necessary.

6. Clarification of the number of working steps in which the material is to be dealt with. The number of working steps depends entirely on the disposition of the material on the lesson sheet.

7. A clear elaboration of the ideological insights inherent in the material to be presented. These ideological insights give the lesson its educational value and must guide the actions of the ⚡⚡-man.

In terms of historical topics, this means:

When discussing the subject matter, the leader must not only focus on the historical events, but must also uncover the political driving forces that brought about the historical events. He must reveal where these driving forces come from and to which conditions and views they are bound, whether they work for or against us.

This also means awakening in the ⚡⚡-man a sense of political responsibility, political obedience, community discipline and a willingness to take action. The art of education begins when the educator transforms the facts of history into ideological insights and into wilful and political impulses that drive the ⚡⚡-man to fight fanatically for the Reich and to defeat the enemy.

In terms of life studies, this means:

The ⚡⚡-man must obey the laws of life of his people and the laws of the order and learn to prove his whole responsibility towards family, ⚡⚡, folk and Reich and his whole racial pride.

This means further: to recognise our common blood as the living, natural and creative basis of the Reich, which is to be defended to the last in defiance of all plutocracy and Bolshevism. Here, too, the supreme law is to convert the knowledge gained into a fanatical will for unrestricted victory.

8. An emphasis on ideological theses which can be derived as an extract from the thought content of the subject matter. In some cases, these theses are included in the lesson plans. Such a thesis can be a word of the Führer or a well-known National Socialist, but can also be coined by the ⚡⚡-men themselves.

If possible, these theses must be made a fixed part of knowledge.

9. A practical application of the ideological knowledge. The reality of life in the past and especially in the present must be examined in terms of ideological and political tensions. Where was action taken in the spirit of our worldview or where was it violated? (Let the consequences be recognised.)

Finally, the ⚡⚡-man must learn to decide instinctively for the Führer's political measures and for the necessity of our struggle. He must measure the National Socialist aspirations against those of his opponents and, by means of examples and comparisons, come to the conclusion *that there is no salvation for us outside the National Socialist worldview and no German or European future without final victory.*

B. Draft of a practical lesson

1. Objective: topic.

2. Presentation of the subject matter (using existing visual aids).

Section 1: Lecture: (or discussion)

Educational talk: Factual clarification of the subject matter and explanation of the causal connections. If possible, highlighting a National Socialist thesis.

Summary: The material is presented by one person in a coherent speech under a sharply formulated heading. This can be given by the unit leader in the first period, but must generally be found by the listeners themselves after the teaching discussion.

All sections are treated in the same way.

3. Worldview evaluation of the material.

Highlighting of ideological knowledge. See VI, A, 7.

4. Elaboration of ideological theses on the basis of the whole subject matter. Subject matter see VI, A,8

5 Practical application to life. See VI, A, 9.

Practice will show that not all subject matter can be treated uniformly according to this "*outline of a practical lesson*", but that the teaching discussion, in considering the causal connections, often involuntarily touches at the same time on ideological knowledge, ideological principles and also practical application related to the reality of life. This is not dangerous in itself, but rather quite natural. The sketch is not intended to be understood as a fixed rule, but to show what has to be done in order to impart clear insights to the ⚡⚡-man, to consolidate them in his consciousness and to make them an unalterable obligation for the ⚡⚡-man's life practice.

Finally, the necessity of the so-called follow-up is pointed out. After each lesson, the unit leader gives a clear account of his own work. If he has been successful, he must clarify the reasons for his success. But it is much more important to get to the bottom of any failures. The unit leader should never look for the cause of failure in the ⚡⚡-men, but always in himself. In all cases, honest follow-up will be fruitful for later lessons and will bring the unit leader closer to the art of teaching and educating.

SS HANDBLÄTTER

FÜR DEN WELTANSCHAULICHEN UNTERRICHT

Lesson 1

Only the National Socialist worldview secures us a life appropriate to our species.

"National Socialism is a cool doctrine of reality of the sharpest scientific knowledge and its mental expression. By having opened up and opening up the heart of our people for this teaching, we do not wish to fill it with a mysticism which lies outside the purpose and aim of our teaching."

Adolf Hitler

I. What does Weltanschauung mean?

It is necessary to explain this concept first, especially in view of the fact that the present war has become a total confrontation of different worldviews. "Weltanschauung" means, first of all, simply looking at the world. In a broader sense, a worldview is the epitome of all thoughts and ideas of a community of people about the world and life. Every worldview is conditioned and shaped by the whole of human existence, such as race, upbringing, environment and experience. Worldviews are therefore expressions of human life forms and vice versa.

"The very word 'worldview' contains the solemn proclamation of the decision to base all actions on a certain initial view. Such a view can be right or wrong. It is the starting point for taking a stand on all phenomena and processes of life and thus a binding and obligatory law for every action. The more such a conception coincides with the natural laws of organic life, the more useful its conscious application will be for the life of a people".

II. The National Socialist Worldview

The National Socialist worldview has emerged from the knowledge of the basic racial, blood and moral forces of the German people. It has grown out of the uncorrupted and healthiest elements of the people themselves. It is therefore not a frigid ethnic force that is based on a practical, communication, but rather on the arts and crafts of the German people.

The life of the German people has restored to itself its very own order through the National Socialist worldview. Consequently, this world-view cannot be chosen or grasped by every human being, but it takes possession of all those who are bound to the laws of the people and of life, and it forces them under its spell.

III. National and Social Community

The combination of the national with the socialist thought has given the party its name and allows us to speak of the National Socialist worldview.

The Führer said:

"The great cultural achievement of mankind has at all times been the supreme achievements of the community life of the people, of the race; they are therefore in their emergence and in their image the expression of the community soul and ideals."

National Socialism thus professes the natural conception of life that is in our blood and that has always belonged to our Germanic ancestors. But it also overcame the individualistic-materialistic ideas of liberalism and Marxism.

With the recognition of the idea of a blood community and the establishment of a socialist community, the Germans became a nation.

"With a great deal of care for honour and freedom" is the necessary battle cry of a new generation that wants to build a new empire and is looking for standards by which it can judge its actions and aspirations in a fruitful way. This call is nationalist and socialist!"

Alfred Rosenberg:"Myth of the XXth Century", p. 534

IV. National Socialism - a natural worldview

If we trace our history back to the earliest Germanic prehistoric times, the following expressions of life of the Germanic-German man become apparent:

1. His upright, proud and blood-conscious nature, the nobility and warriorism which finds its expression in soldierly toughness and determination and his courage in battle, in his high conception of honour and freedom, loyalty and obedience and his leadership

2. His high sense of community (family, clan, people) and his willingness to make any sacrifice for these blood communities.

3. His pleasant and hard-working nature, his attachment to the land, his love for the soil.

4. His great intelligence, which made him the founder of the cultures and states of the West and thus, from antiquity to the present day, the regulating and determining factor in the co-existence of peoples.

5. His profound belief.

This is the foundation of National Socialism. It professes the high values of Germanic humanity, whereby it must be expressly emphasised that the idealism of our conception has nothing to do with rapture and phantasmagoria. National Socialism is life in the blood of the national community and a service to the people as if it were the only law for every German man. It is the life of blood and honour. A main component of the National Socialist doctrine is the demand for freedom for the national community and hatred against oneself.

With this basic view of life, National Socialism stands in irreconcilable opposition to the worldview of materialism, whose bearers are the Jew and his vassal peoples.

This war represents the inexorable opposition between these two worldviews.

"National Socialism realises in the reality of politics what we look upon with a believing heart and recognise with a courageous spirit as necessary and right. It is the doctrine of the destiny of our people. It is the mastery of the world of inheritance and the environment. It puts the myth of blood and honour into words. It directs our eyes back to the essential events of blood and soil. It directs our thinking, faith and action back to the eternal order of the world within us and the world around us. It gives us the confidence and the possibility to reverently penetrate into the lawfulness of omnipotence and to align the order, which is set and shaped for us by human beings, according to its laws, so that it becomes lawful according to nature and life. For only then will the future of our people be secure, clear and certain."

Stengel v . Rutkowski : On Omnipotence and the Order of Life

V. The Importance of Personality

If we see the individual as a serving member of the national community, this does not mean that he or she is absorbed into the masses. Genuine national community cannot grow out of masses, but only out of strong personalities. A healthy forest needs strong trees! The National Socialist thus emphasises the value of personality. However, this does not mean the value of the individual detached from all ties for its own sake, since such an individual does not exist in reality. It exists only as a bloodless thought construct and contradicts the laws of life according to which man is born into the naturally grown orders of family, clan and people.

National Socialism wants to create a personality which is fully developed in all its abilities and aptitudes, conscious of its blood, strong-willed, and firm in character, and which is of the highest service to the Folk. The means of creating this type of person is education in the spirit of the National Socialist worldview. The prerequisite for this is the preservation of purity and the higher development of our blood through breeding.

The Führer said:

"We have the great task of deepening the strong faith in the Folk Community more and more and of bringing out the value of personality more and more clearly."

VI. The Struggle as a National Socialist Law of Life

We value struggle as an irrevocable law of life, for only in eternal struggle, the prerequisite of all selection, do personalities and hard people grow. Only in struggle is greatness born.

"Whoever wants to live, let him fight, and whoever does not want to fight in this world of eternal wrestling of eternal struggle, does not deserve to live."

Adolf Hitler

The German man shapes his life in struggle, struggle accompanies his entire existence: struggle with himself, struggle with fate, struggle with the hostile environment. In tenacious struggle he masters fate and fights for himself and his people the way of life that is inherent in their nature and thus intended by God. Struggle is the divine law for German man to form and educate himself, to toughen himself. *"Praise be to that which makes hard."* That is why he rejects the hitherto taught principle of humble submission to fate.

Struggle and toughness are the main elements of National Socialism. It is therefore the worldview of the strong, the combative human being. National Socialism springs from genuine soldiering. With its basic militant trait, it is a solid worldview. The sacrificial commitment of the soldier, however, is the most visible socialism. The soldier is the first socialist of the Reich. It is precisely the soldier who must accept National Socialism with special readiness in his heart and be its most fanatical confessor.

The soldier is the first socialist in the Reich and must embrace National Socialism in his heart and be its most loyal proponent. From this militant attitude, National Socialism abhors an effeminate life of ease. It is the mortal enemy of egoism and materialism, which lead to a dissolute life. It demands simplicity, plainness and straightforwardness in the conduct of life. The peasant strong and genuine and the soldierly hardiness should fill every German, regardless of whether he serves his people in the city or in the country, with a weapon or at the workbench.

"If the fight for a worldview is not led by heroes willing to sacrifice, there will be no more death-defying fighters in a short time."

Adolf Hitler: "Mein Kampf", p. 114

VII. Commitment to Honour and Loyalty

We profess honour and loyalty, both of which belong indissolubly together. The concept of honour is the centre of Germanic existence in general. The lives of our ancestors revolved around honour and glory, freedom, bravery and pride.   Their lives were always pure and great as long as honour took precedence.

"Germanic Europe endowed the world with the most luminous ideal of humanity: with the doctrine of the value of character as the basis of all morality, with the hymn to the highest values of the Nordic being, to the idea of freedom of conscience and honour."

Alfred Rosenberg

In recent centuries, the high concept of honour has been strongly affected by the ideas of humility and humanity. The Führer made honour the focal point of German life.

Honour is the inner law, the conscience, which dictates all our actions and our attitude towards the national community. It is never related to itself alone, but finds its actual interpretation in the relationship of the ego to the community. The Germanic-German concept of marriage allows the self to take a back seat in favour of the honour of the people. Our National Socialist worldview, with its life and death values, is based on honour. The socialist idea of voluntary service for the people and the striving to keep our blood pure develops from honour. But he who has honour in his body will never abandon his comrade, his people or even his leader. For from honour grows loyalty.

VIII. My honour is loyalty

To the ᛋᛋ-man the Führer gave the slogan which obliges him to be the first soldier of National Socialism for now and all the future: *"ᛋᛋ-man your Honour is Loyalty!"*

Many things on this Earth can be forgiven, but one thing never can: disloyalty. The loyalty we have sworn to the Führer must be as sacred to us as loyalty to the German people, its will and its ways, as loyalty to blood, to our ancestors and grandchildren, loyalty to our kin, loyalty to comrades and loyalty to the immutable laws of decency, cleanliness and chivalry. In the raising of honour and duty, the ideal of the German people is expressed.

"Let us all profess these principles and close the great ring of our community, strong in our trust in our people, fulfilled in our faith in our mission and ready to make any sacrifice that the Almighty demands of us. Then Germany, the National Socialist Third Reich, will pass through this time of

hardship, sorrow and worry, armed with that metal which alone enables the knight to stand without fear or blame in the struggle against death and the devil: the core of the iron heart."

Adolf Hitler

SS HANDBLÄTTER
FÜR DEN WELTANSCHAULICHEN UNTERRICHT

The laws of life - the basis of our National Socialist worldview

"By attempting to rebel against the iron logic of nature, man comes into struggle with the principles to which he himself owes his very existence as a human being. Thus, his action against nature must lead to his own downfall."

Mein Kampf

The Laws of Life

Life on this earth is governed by iron laws: Birth, becoming, growing, maturing, ageing and death outline a part and are familiar to us consciously and unconsciously. These laws apply to all life, to man, to death and to life. In addition, we must recall everything that is described by the following words: Struggle for existence, selection, fruitfulness, race, heredity, Impact of the environment and development.

Struggle for existence

Every living being has to fight for food and reproduction. It is necessary to assert oneself in the struggle for existence. The struggle for existence is determined by three groups:

1. Natural enemies,

3. Own conspecifics.

In the struggle for existence, the one who, for whatever reason, eliminates those less fit to live in this struggle asserts himself.

"Whoever wants to live, let him fight, and whoever does not want to fight in this world of eternal struggle does not deserve life."

"Mein Kampf".

The struggle for existence in human life must not be confused with social looseness, poverty, exploitation and so on. These are expressions of social injustice, of anti-socialism, of degradation. Life has added the natural sense of community or community instinct to this law.

Pacifism represents the strongest negation of the law of struggle.

What does selection mean?

The struggle for existence causes a constant selection of the best. Those who assert themselves and prevail are preserved and can reproduce, while the unfit, the unworthy of life, are weeded out

Anyone who is too weak cannot become a blacksmith. Anyone with clumsy fingers cannot successfully pursue the profession of a precision mechanic. Many professions require a special intelligence. Thus, it can be said in general that the members of almost all professions represent selection groups in different directions in each case.

What does fertility mean?

For some species, their fertility is the only effective weapon in the struggle for existence. Only when they appear en masse can they hold their own. Fertility also plays a major role in the conflict between peoples. The danger that the fertility of one people can pose to another is shown by the severe conflict in the East.

Especially the high-value peoples must observe this law, otherwise they are doomed to perish.

"But the end will be that such a people will one day be deprived of its existence in this world; for man can certainly defy the eternal laws of the will to perpetuate himself for a certain time, but sooner or later revenge will come. A stronger generation will chase away the weak, since the urge to live in its last form will break all ridiculous fetters of a so-called humanity of the individual again and again, in order to let the humanity of nature take its place, which destroys weakness in order to give place to strength. Whoever, therefore, wants to secure the existence of the German people by means of a self-limitation of its increase, robs it of its future."

Mein Kampf"

What does race mean?

Race is a group of living beings with the same hereditary basic characteristics. The Führer brought us the realisation of the importance of race, the knowledge and value of the importance of blood.

His teaching states:

1. That mankind consists of different races;

2. That each people can live fully only according to its blood laws;

3. That our people are a blood community of predominantly Nordic blood;

4. That our people must live according to laws which correspond to Nordic blood;

5. That world history, apart from the struggle for living space, represents the tension between the racial-psychological worldviews.

It is a fact of experience and observation that people who have the characteristics of a human race are different (Negroes - Whites). The difference of people is a fact. The closer people are related to each other (family resemblance, tribal resemblance), the smaller the difference. Each race has characteristics that are adapted to its living conditions and thus to each other; it forms a harmonious unity

This harmony is naturally disturbed by conflict, resulting in a lack of harmony. Countries with a distinctly mixed-race population (America) cannot pursue a steady, purposeful and clear policy because of their racial divisions. They are constantly interrupted in their development by uprisings, revolutions and power struggles. In contrast, peoples with a racially unified leadership are essentially stable in their development.

The history of mankind is the history of racial struggles. The history of a people is its racial fate. If the history-making race perishes, the country becomes desolate, it becomes historyless.

"All the great cultures of the past perished only because the original creative race died of blood poisoning."

"No, there is only one most sacred human right, and this right is at the same time the most sacred obligation, namely: to see to it that the blood is preserved pure, in order to give the possibility of a nobler development of these beings by preserving the best of humanity."

"Mein Kampf"

What do we need to know about heredity?

Heredity means preservation of the good, but also of all that is bad. Through it you pass on your abilities and qualities to your children. The life laws of race and selection cannot be understood without the fact of heredity. Although this law was considered to be valid for animals and plants, opponents of this relationship want to grant humans a special position. Human heredity, however, has proved on the basis of the results of research into races, families and twins that the law of heredity naturally also applies to man. Heredity shows us that we cannot go beyond the scope of the inherited characteristics given to us. Here man is subject to a natural limitation. Heredity is destiny.

What does environment mean?

By environment we mean all the forces that act on the being from outside, i.e.: environment, climate, education, etc. The hereditary disposition is the determining factor; the environment cannot change it. In contrast to the theory of heredity is the theory of the environment, which interprets all cultural phenomena as an effect of the environment. Marxism has its essential foundation in the environmental theory. Among the followers of the environmental theory, education in particular is given great importance.

However, it is only possible within the framework of inheritance. You can't make a hero out of a cowardly child, or an intellectual out of a fool. The environment does not form, but in the long run has the effect of selecting, i.e., sifting and breeding.

"However much, for example, the soil is able to influence men, the result of the influence will always be different, according to the races under consideration. The low fertility of a habitat may spur one race to the highest achievements, in another it will only bring about the cause of abject poverty and finite malnutrition with all its consequences. It is always the internal disposition of the people that determines the nature of the effects of external influences. What leads to starvation in some educates others to hard work."

"Mein Kampf"

As the earth has gradually evolved, so has life on it. Every living being reaches in an unbroken chain of reproduction and multiplication into the most distant primeval times. The fact of development in nature disturbs dogmatic worldviews. The idea of development has overthrown the idea of creation, and therein lies its political significance, also in the ideological field.

The life-law worldview

"I say it here prophetically, just as the realisation of the orbit of the earth around the sun led to a revolutionary reshaping of the general worldview, so the blood and race doctrine of the National Socialist movement will result in a revolution of knowledge and thus of the picture of the history of the human past and future."

"Mein Kampf"

What do you need to know about racial thought?

The idea of race embraces all aspects of life. It gives you the freedom of action to make the right choice of marriage and thus determines your and your children's, families and siblings' fate.

It gives you a firm position in your people, your state, your continent and in the community of nations.

It demands of you your own life and work and thus promises you a very happy life.

Biological thinking creates reasonable standards for evaluating things. It gives you the strength to make clear decisions, shows you what you can and should do and thus leads to the formation of your personality.

The development of racial thought always leads to the organic order of life and not to institutionalism, ecclesiastical or political systems.

Racial thinking affirms the natural life and the duty of God to the people, not only of the individual but also of the nations.

It promises to each his own and denies unjustified claims of individuals.

The opponents of the idea of race

One opponent of the idea of race wants equality between people. Such a principle, because it is un-biological and thus un-natural, creates for him the tensions, desires and claims necessary for him, the dissatisfaction and thus the prerequisite of his power.

Thus, the other opponent wants the spiritual binding to life-hostile laws dogmas by exploiting the religious feelings of humanity and thus first creates the prerequisite of life-legally not necessary existence.

Thus, a third opponent, Bolshevism, deliberately destroys all expressions of the natural order of life, such as family, the joy of children, of one's own home, the attachment to home and clan, the bond with clan and ancestors. He wants the complete eradication of all natural facts and thus creates the prerequisite for the implementation of his plans. Today we see from our life-law thinking why Bolshevism, in order to preserve itself, must act in this way.

Reference :

1) SS-Man and blood question.

2) Racial politics.

SS
HANDBLÄTTER
FÜR DEN WELTANSCHAULICHEN UNTERRICHT

Lesson 3

We fight for the eternity of our people

"Our National Socialist programme substitutes for the liberalist concept of the individual and the Marxist concept of humanity the blood-bound and soil-bound people. A very simple and lapidary sentence, alone of tremendous implications. For the first time, perhaps, since there has been a history of mankind, the realisation has been directed in this country that of all the tasks set before us, the most honourable, and therefore the most sacred to man, is the preservation of the God-given blood-bound species."

Mein Kampf

National Socialism brought Germany rebirth after the fall of 1918. It has reborn the German life according to our principles. The Führer created the Reich and united in it all ethnic groups of German blood.

Racial science became the basis for the development of the nation and the state from the realisation that all values and cultural achievements are linked to heredity.

The doctrine of the equality of all human beings became the teaching of the race is not confined to the heredity.

The Folk

The folk have grown from the forces of their blood, which are passed on through heredity and selected by the conditions of the environment. For only the most capable prove themselves in the struggle for life. They alone have the courage to pass on life to numerous descendants, while the less life-affirming, out of their fear of the severity of life's struggle, believe they can ease the conditions of life by having few children. Their hereditary dispositions are thus gradually eliminated from the totality of the folk. In this way, the existing hereditary dispositions form the natural stock of a people, which can either be maintained, improved or worsened by reproduction. We must always be aware of this divinely ordained law of life and behave according to it, because our attitude is crucial for the health and integrity of our people.

We therefore demand respect for the hereditary values of our nation.

We recognise the importance of the rule of law as necessary

We recognise the importance of the environment of the nation.

We demand a world that has grown up in the folk and a knowledge of God that we can understand from our national character. We demand a national politics, a legal and economic order that is in keeping with the times; an art that has grown in the folk and the community and is supported by it; we want a language that proclaims our national nature, and a view of history that illustrates to us the struggle for existence of the different generations of our people.

The orientation of the people

Essential for the preservation or promotion of a certain racial form is, apart from the basic preservation of good hereditary dispositions, the shaping of an environment which is favourable to this "race". This can only be achieved if there is a conscious shaping of the people's community towards this goal (breeding goal) and if the bearers of this community live according to it.

The preservation of the people

"For the first time in this Reich it is possible for man to turn the gift of knowledge and insight bestowed upon him by the Almighty to those questions which are of more tremendous importance for the preservation of his existence than all victorious wars or successful economic battles! The greatest revolution of National Socialism is to have torn open the gate of knowledge for the fact that all the faults and errors of man are temporal and thus capable of being improved again, except for one: the error about the importance of the preservation of his blood, of his kind and thus of the form given to him by God and of the being given to him by God."

" Mein Kampf"

We know from the laws of life and history that people do not die out, but are born out, i.e., only the people who forget their task of passing on their life to the coming generations sink back into nothingness.

The Folk State

The neglect of blood is the cause of the downfall; the decline of the population, the oppression of the people, the mismanagement of the environment and the lack of proper propagation are the dangers and causes of the change in the overall picture.

The eternal folk

We are fighting for our women and children and thus for the eternal life of our folk, not only in the present great struggle, but always and everywhere. That is why we have to work for an order of life for our nation that also ensures eternal life from within. This can only be an order that preserves and promotes the good and valuable life, but suppresses and eliminates the inferior and harmful, an order that allows the clans of the people to grow in the soil of the homeland.

The fight against inferiority

Legal measures can lead to the elimination of unwanted, diseased genetic material. *"Law for the Prevention of Hereditary Diseases."* Furthermore, preventive detention of habitual criminals can keep them from reproducing. *"Laws against dangerous habitual offenders and on measures of security and correction"*. The *"Nuremberg Laws"* for the protection of German blood and German honour are also the guarantee that foreign blood mixing does not change the overall character of the genetic traits of the folk.

"The demand that defective human beings be prevented from procreating other equally defective human beings is a demand of the clearest reason and, if carried out according to plan, represents the most humane act of humanity. It will spare millions of unfortunate people undeserved suffering, but will subsequently lead to the health of the population to rise."

"Mein Kampf"

To promote good genes

In addition to measures to eliminate undesirable genetic material, laws to promote good genetic material serve to directly increase good genetic material. The *"Marriage Health Act"* for the protection of the hereditary health of the German people prevents the mixing of good hereditary traits with undesirable ones. The *"Betrothal and Marriage Order"* of the ⚡⚡ serves not only to ensure timely education in the examination of the marriage partner, but also to prevent the spread of undesirable hereditary traits. *The ""Mother Protection Act"* serves to safeguard the expectant mother and the undisturbed care of the infant.

What does the term "breeding" mean?

The idea of breeding was something our ancestors took for granted. Family or clan leaders ensured that the best and most talented of both sexes were kept. The legal measures of a promoting or preventing nature alone are not enough to keep a people in the same species forever.

Choice of spouse

Every marriage of a family member means the inclusion of a new hereditary property in the clan. Therefore, the choice of a mate is of crucial importance not only for the unmarried but also for their descendants.

The choice of a wife gives the man the only opportunity in life to influence or develop the heredity of the next generation. Health or illness, talent or incapacity of the offspring are decided by the choice of wife. In this decisive step, it is not position or wealth that must be the deciding factor, but only the spiritual and physical ability. It is clear that the one who is certain to be the bearer of unhealthy hereditary traits must renounce. The choice of a wife is the most important step in the course of life and for the transmission of life. Therefore, it is necessary that all life-law findings are observed with the utmost rigour in this decision.

Summary of our demands

Take care of your health and, as long as you are in the years of development, abstain from stimulants (alcohol, nicotine) and sexual activity. (The Nordic person in particular generally only reaches full maturity late in life).

Marry as early as possible. Only then will you be able to enjoy family happiness to the full.

Do not marry a woman from another tribe. You are responsible to your people and your descendants for keeping the blood pure.

Do not marry a sick wife. Otherwise, you will be responsible for the sickness of your own children and grandchildren.

Choose only a fully healthy wife. The true picture of your future wife's health and qualities will show you her personality.

Your wife should be at least as valuable as you are. Try to make your and your children's environment as natural as possible.

Try to create a natural environment for you and your children, because unfavourable hereditary dispositions are almost always hidden from you and then develop twice as much in your children.

Only the largest possible number of children can guarantee the development of your inheritance. The most famous men in particular often come from families with many children.

In addition to the professional fulfilment of duty, there must also be biological achievement. Only the two together result in life achievement.

Remember that nature demands a struggle for what is valuable. Nothing that is easy to achieve fulfils the conditions of a selection. Only what you achieve through hard struggle makes you truly happy. First and foremost is the preservation and promotion of our people and their nationhood. Our lives and struggles are dedicated to this task.

"National Socialism has neither the individual nor humanity as the starting point for its considerations, its statements and resolutions. It consciously places at the centre of all its thinking: the folk."

"The great cultural achievements of mankind have at all times been the supreme achievements of the communal life of the people, of the race; they are therefore in their emergence and in their image the expression of the communal soul and ideals."

"Mein Kampf"

The higher development of our folk

Life-law thinking recognises the development in nature. This obliges us to strive for a higher development of our folk. The most important basic law for the order of life of our folk is as follows: What is important is what is conducive to the development of the German people. What is immoral is what is detrimental to the development of the German nation.

Reference :

1) ⚡⚡-Man and the question of blood

2) Racial policy

3) Curriculum for ideological education

HANDBLÄTTER
FÜR DEN WELTANSCHAULICHEN UNTERRICHT

Lesson 4

As National Socialists, we believe in a divine world order

"Our creed exclusively means: cultivating the natural and thus also the divinely willed. Our humility is the unconditional bowing to the divine laws of existence that are becoming known to us and their respect. Our prayer is: Brave fulfilment of the resulting duties."

The Führer at the 1938 National Party Congress

I. Are we godless?

We have heard this accusation again and again today and in previous years. We often clenched our fists in silent bitterness at such abuse on the part of a group of people who believed they could criticize us from the security of a supposed belief. If one was forced to admit the successes of National Socialism in all areas, then the last "but" was always the refuge in the argument of godlessness. We have learned that such people are not to be debated with. We are towering above such slander. Today we no longer think of talking to everyone about our faith. Let's look at the Führer. Who has not been moved again and again in his great speeches by his holy faith in an omnipotent providence? How often has the Führer confessed that in all his actions he is one with providence, he feels himself to be its appointed tool.

"I, too, am religious, and deeply religious, and I believe that Providence weighs people and does not determine to greater things those who cannot stand before the test of providence, but breaks in it. It is a natural necessity that only the strongest remain in the selection."

The Führer on November 8, 1943

If all words and concepts are unable to express our faith, then the work of the Führer proves to us that we are now with our faith in a genuine God – consciousness, a deep penetration.

II. Are we fighting the Church?

Together with the first, this reproach was repeatedly made to us by internal enemies; our external enemies accuse us of this again today in the most hateful way. The Führer has emphasized endlessly that the Church and her priests always enjoy the protection of the state, provided that they devote themselves exclusively to pastoral care and do not act contrary to the political will of the people. The controversy of the individual with an old doctrine of the faith is only too often and too gladly equated with "state-tolerated" attacks against the church. Basically, it can be said that at all times and among all peoples there have been upheavals in the religious sphere; one will not want to deny our time the right to one of our being to seek proper faith in God.

III. The idea of race - the supreme thesis of the National Socialist worldview

Our concept of race is only an expression of a worldview that recognizes a divine commandment in the higher development of man.

"If the world is God's creation, the laws of nature according to which the universe is transformed and developed must be divine laws. The laws that are of particular validity for us humans are, however, those that shape our hereditary world and our environment. Therefore, for us the knowledge of race is the highest knowledge. Everything else has to be based on it. So, if life, race, work, nature, homeland are high and supreme values for us, it is not out of arbitrariness, but because through all these things the way to God, to the meaning of life, to a life-appropriate one, order, morality and faith"

(Stengel - v. Rutkowski:" On omnipotence and order of life ")

We believe that the races are parts of the divine world order.

Racial care, racial purity and racial selection are therefore divine commandments. The purer the races are in themselves, the purer and richer they will be able to develop their inherent abilities and aptitudes, the greater will be their contributions to the fulfilment of the meaning of the human order.

IV. The folk as a member of the order of creation

The starting point of National Socialist teaching is the folk. In them we recognize the visible workings of a divine will to order. That is why the fiercest opponent of National Socialism is any form of international equalisation, whether of a political or religious nature. Because only through belonging and confession to the folk does the individual stand under the true law of God. This law obliges him to use his life in accordance with the divine order. That is why for us National Socialists a violation of the moral principles of our folk, against loyalty and obedience means a real blasphemy.

A man's greatest good is his people.

"My will, that must be the confession of all of us - is your faith! My faith is to me - just like you - everything in this world! But the highest thing that God has given me in this world is my people! My faith rests in him, I serve him with my will, and I give him my life. "

The Führer on May 1st, 1935.

V. Clan and family as divine institutions for the preservation of life

"Caring for what is natural and thus also what is divinely willed is our most sacred task," says the Führer. Since family and clan are the actual bearers of the people, the bond to them means service to the people, worship. This service is free from any mystical semi-darkness of ritual acts. The high points of life, the birth, naming, engagement, wedding and death become a celebration and festive event in the family and clan community alone. You too, in the midst of which steps on the path of man only gain the highest meaning, also shape the forms of these events. We set family and clan as a divine order against uprooting and mass growth and the homelessness of a disenfranchised international proletariat.

VI. Real faith versus pious mendacity

The opponent tries only too gladly to accuse us of religious crimes or to accuse us of "paganism". But he hypocritically describes the desecration of European cathedrals, monuments and cultural sites as necessary for the destruction of barbarism. We oppose this will to destroy with the unshakable belief in a just, divine order. The opponent will be mistaken about the strength of our faith.

From the National Socialist worldview we have grown the belief in a meaningful world order. It is the backbone of our political will, which emerged victorious from the time of struggle of the movement and which will also end this struggle victoriously. To those who, in a narrow-minded piety dominated solely by dogma, fear that we might lose the war because we are supposedly godless, may be told: the crowning glory of the National Socialist worldview lies in the deep-rooted faith in an all-encompassing Godly order. We only recognise it as the supreme law for the life of peoples.

"Religions only have meaning if they serve to preserve the living substance of a human race. For once the peoples as such have perished, neither the religions nor the states remain as eternal phenomena."

The Führer at the 1935 National Party Congress

"A people to be one, that is the religion of our time; through this faith you must be united and strong, by overcoming the devil and the oils! Leave all the little religions and do the duty of the only highest, and high above the Pope and Luther, you unite in them in one faith"

Ernst Moritz Arndt

SS
HANDBLÄTTER
FÜR DEN WELTANSCHAULICHEN UNTERRICHT

Lesson 5

We are Socialists

"By trying to find someone born in my people for every function of life in order to transfer responsibility to them in this area regardless of their previous economic or social origins, I am acting in the interests of everyone. But if the word socialism is supposed to have any meaning at all, then it can only have that, in iron justice, that is, the deepest insight, to burden everyone with the preservation of the whole that which corresponds to him thanks to his innate disposition and thus his values!"

The Führer in his closing speech at the 1933 party congress

What does the word "Socialism" mean?

The word socialism is derived from Sozius = comrade, journeyman. National Socialism = National Folk community!

National Socialism means justice within the national folk community in the sense that the performance of the individual for this community is the sole yardstick for his evaluation.

Why are we Socialists?

Because genuine socialism is an expression of our racial substance and therefore aims at the healthy preservation of our blood community.

Because only a just social order secures the future of the German people and of Europe.

Because we have learned from the past and its mistakes.

What were the mistakes?

The German people did not form a closed community; Compared to other peoples, it had exemplary social settings, health insurance, accident insurance, disability insurance, employee insurance, old-age provision, but as a people it was divided and fragmented. The true community feeling was missing.

A deep gulf separated the state and the people. Social institutions alone do not guarantee socialism. The people must be educated to think, want and act socially.

Materialistic thinking prevailed. The rise of technology was not in the service of the folk community and social justice, but was a means of exploitation by Jews and international capital.

Concentration of wealth in the hands of a few: and for millions whose standard of living was constantly kept low by greed for profit. This justified the workers' unhappiness.

The misery of unemployment - The state as a handout provider (the "dole" office)

The prejudice against manual labour. - Decline in the valuation of agricultural labour. - Decline of the peasantry.

The labourers and the workers became the victims of the Jew's agitation.   The divided people became the plaything and the object of exploitation of foreign powers. Europe was kept in constant turmoil and embroiled in ever new wars by the intrigues and machinations of the plutocrats. The class struggle was repeated here in the struggle of the peoples.

What does our socialism want?

The party programme demands:

Point 9: All citizens must have the same rights and obligations.

Point 10: The first duty of every citizen must be to work mentally or physically. The activity of the individual must not go against the interests of the general public, but must be carried out within the framework of the whole for the benefit of all.

The idea of class struggle is replaced by a new image of life: the folk-community. It is the topmost value = National Socialism!

The folk community secures the life and continuation of the people and thus also every national comrade.

Every person should shape their own destiny on their own responsibility. The folk community, however, is responsible for ensuring that none of its members get into trouble through no fault of their own.

The folk community knows no social prejudices. It excludes any kind of class and group egoism.

The folk community imposes an obligation on each and every one of them. The measure for this is disposition, talent and the ability for the people: the right man in the right place. All training and development opportunities are open to every national comrade that corresponds to their talents. The obligation to work corresponds to the right to fair wages.

The Fuhrer said: *"Only when a nation is healthy in body and soul in all its members can the joy of belonging to it rise to that lofty feeling that we call national pride."* "Mein Kampf , Page 474

The folk-community guarantees security in old age, security in the event of illness, disability and maternity, as well as the livelihood of widows and orphans. (Opposite example: Britain.)

Social justice and the principle of achievement raise their demands for all forms of labour and service. The service for the community determines the social rank and the position of the personality. Privileges that are not based on personal commitment are rejected.

The Führer: *"Honour the work and respect the worker."*

The folk , to which both are obliged, stands above employers and employees.

National Socialism opposes the idea of charity with the obligation to stand up for the community with every sacrifice.

German socialism is not an act of charity, but honour and duty, service and sacrifice.

The Führer wrote : *"Whoever loves his people proves it only by the sacrifices he is prepared to make for them. A reason for the pride of the people exists only when one no longer needs to be ashamed of any rank."*

"Mein Kampf", page 474

Blood and soil are the foundations of socialism. A healthy countryside must form the basis of the socialist order in agriculture as well.

Our socialism realises the principle of freedom of movement. The soldier is the highest expression of socialist will. The soldierly community is built on comradeship, loyalty, performance and sacrifice.

The Führer: *"You are not born a socialist, you have to be educated to become one."*

The socialism of our enemies

"Comparing the social policies of the enemy with ours is just an insult"

Dr. Goebbels.

The enemy's political system is anti-social and unfair.

Bolshevism, an invention of Jewish brains, claims that it alone eliminated exploitation in this world by liquidating private property.

In reality, Bolshevism is the most blatant form of social injustice and exploitation and only serves Judaism's striving for world domination. Bolshevism means:

Destruction of personality and race: the peasant should become agricultural workers, the worker proletarians, the countries labour provinces for international Jewry.

The non-Bolshevik people were "liquidated". The Soviet Union was hermetically sealed off from the outside world. The residents only learned what was going on in the world what was wanted to be told to them most powerful policy of deception in world history. Since there were no possibilities of comparison, the Russian got a completely wrong picture of his country's progress.

The contempt and gagging of small and weak peoples: they are raped in the Bolshevik sense. (The fate of the Baltic states after the invasion of the Bolsheviks.)

Lenin wrote: "*Through complete tyranny we will push humanity down to the ultimate level of equality which alone makes humanity suitable to become an easy-to-use, uniform tool of our power*"

In Britain and the United States there are the plutocrats: the economy servants of money, the people only servants of the economy.

The United States with inexhaustible resources, which could have been of great value to the community, are underutilized. The army of millions of the unemployed stand witness to this.

England, the most socially backward state in the world.

Today's demands of Britons were carried out with us fifty years ago.

The slums in London.

Strikes and unrest among the workers out of dissatisfaction.

The successes of German socialism

Eliminate unemployment.

Right to work. - Fair wages. - Curbing high profits through taxes.

The National Socialist People's Welfare. The promotion of the family :

Marital Loans. - child allowances. - training aid. - tax breaks.

Generous help for mother and child. - kindergartens. - Community care stations. – Children's Education.

Developing effective youth through a healthy upbringing. Prohibition of child labour. - Law on the protection of minors.

Creation of opportunities for advancement regardless of status, profession and assets.

National Socialist Educational Institutions, Adolf Hitler Schools, Order Castles, supportive professional education for adults, introduction of the concept of competition. (Model companies, competition between all working Germans, the company suggestion scheme.)

The measures for the recovery of the German peasantry (Reich Court of Justice Act).

The introduction of social responsibility (manager, trustee of work).

Securing annual vacation leave.

Creation of healthy housing, improvement of the landscape of cities, living spaces, beauty of work programme

Maintaining sports and physical exercise (Germany's victory at the 1936 Olympics.)

Access to the cultural goods and educational media of the nation (Strength Through Joy movement.).

The war interrupted the steep rise in social development; it hit us in the midst of our economic and social development.

The basic social law in war: Nobody should get rich from war.

The exemplary care of the soldiers' families, the war disabled and bereaved.

Why is the enemy waging war?

The people saw the rise of the German people.

People began to talk about the success of National Socialism. The government of the hostile countries felt the imperative to carry out radical reforms.

The plutocrats feared the upheaval of the capitalist social structure.

The Jews saw their position of power wavering; the hatred they stoked led to war.

The aim of the Jewish world leaders: extermination and annihilation of the German people.

The old social order is felt by a large part of the people in all countries to be inadequate.

The realisation of this socialist order of life is the Reich.

The new European order can only be established through a new sense of community. By professing the idea of the folk community, the folk create the prerequisites for a socialist Europe without proletarians. The concern for social justice is the dominant principle of folkish life.

Socialism in its real form is the highest national livelihood and the deepest source of national power.

German socialism is embodied in the figure of Adolf Hitler: from a simple man of the people he became the leader of the Reich.

The Führer said: *"We have a state in mind where in the future every position should be filled by the most capable son, no matter where he comes from: A state in which birth is nothing and performance and ability is everything."*

References:

"Mein Kampf", p. 474;

 Material collections of the ⚡⚡ main office:

"The way of the NSDAP."

"Americanism, a World Danger," pp. 15, 24, 27, 41;

⚡⚡-Man and the Blood Question", p. 54;

"The Dollar Rolls," pp. 7-10, 35-36;

"Bauerntum", pp. 10, 18, 22, 42;

"The Way to the Reich", p. 94;

"Struggle against Bolshevism".

Lesson 6

This is our Führer Adolf Hitler !

The development of Adolf Hitler and his movement up to the day of the seizure of power in Germany

I. Adolf Hitler's parental home and youth[1]

> ....*"and what then seemed to me to be the hardship of fate, I praise today as the wisdom of providence. When the goddess of need took me in her arms and threatened to break me so often, the will to resist grew and finally the will remained victorious. "*

Adolf Hitler

The ancestors come from the Waldviertel (northwest of today's Lower Danube Gau). They were mostly small farmers or rural artisans.

His father, Alois Hitler, is the first in the line of ancestors to move away from his home area. He was initially a shoemaker and later a customs officer at the then Bavarian-Austrian border in Braunau. The historical significance of Braunau: Here in 1806 the book dealer Palm, who published the pamphlet "Germany in its deepest humiliation", was shot on orders from Napoleon.

Toughness and defiant will emerged early on in the character image of the young Hitler; among his youthful playmates he was the little ringleader who was inspired by an impetuous thirst for action.

At school he is particularly interested in history and geography. Through a history teacher who inspires the young, he learns to understand and grasp the great historical relationships of the peoples according to their senses and thus becomes an ardent nationalist at an early age.

According to his father's wish, Adolf Hitler should become a civil servant like him, but here, too, his strong will prevails: following his deep artistic inclinations, he decides to become an artist.

II. Hard years of apprenticeship in Vienna, which shaped the young Hitler in the strongest way[2]

After the death of his mother, Adolf Hitler moved to Vienna in 1908 and took up life there, left to his own devices.

Adolf Hitler earns his bread here as a baker, painter and artist. During this time, which he lived through with great inner open-mindedness despite great extreme need, he came into contact with the most varied of problems with which he was grappling.

He experienced Vienna at that time as the political centre of a state that contained the most pressing unresolved political and social issues

He realizes that the Austrian Empire of the Habsburg monarchy is completely opposed to the whole of Germany He also recognizes the inevitability of the coming internal disintegration of this multi-ethnic state. These findings reinforce the need for thought of a Greater Germany

He experiences the social problems as a construction worker in the world of the working class with its great mental and material hardships, insecurity of existence, unemployment, housing misery and many other worries.

He sees that selfishness and the ignorance of a liberal civil service are driving the manual workers into the arms of the Marxism and recognises that nationalism and socialism are not opposites, but must flow together in order to prepare the way for a healthy national development

Adolf Hitler also recognises that it is Jewry that uses the intellectual edifice of Marxism in order to realise its plan of world domination by inciting the working class. He becomes an anti-Semite.

Adolf Hitler also got to know the parliamentary economy in Vienna as an institution in which demagogy, empty talk, intrigue , ignorance and, above all, irresponsibility met, and every idea of leadership was put to death.

Thus, the seeds of his great human development were laid in this period of his life in Vienna.

III. The Unknown Soldier of World War[3]

In 1912 Adolf Hitler left Vienna and went to Munich. Here he witnessed the outbreak of the World War.

He registered as a volunteer with the Bavarian Reserve Infantry Regiment No. 16 (List) and was accepted after initial difficulties.

His war comrades and superiors consider Adolf Hitler as an excellent soldier, always ready for the toughest work, who consciously feels himself to be a fighter of the German people.

He received the Iron Cross second class in 1914 and Iron Cross first class in 1918.

Four years without ever having had a vacation in the toughest job, as a messenger on the western front. He is wounded twice. In the autumn of 1918 he suffered severe gas poisoning and was threatened with complete blindness.

Half blind, he experienced the November revolution in the Pasewalk reserve hospital.

During these days, Adolf Hitler is researching the causes of the collapse and vows to take up the struggle against the forces that brought about the decline and makes the decision to become a politician

IV. From the founding of the NSDAP and the SA. to the first Uprising on November 9, 1923[4]

As an education officer, after his release from the hospital, Adolf Hitler met with nationalist groups and labour groups, for example in autumn 1919 he met with the German Workers' Party, of which he became the 7th member .

He becomes the leading organizer and promoter of this group and leads it to ever greater strength.

In the first large-scale meeting on February 24, 1920, Adolf Hitler announced the party's program.

In the spring of 1920, Adolf Hitler named his movement the National Socialist German Workers' Party.

He enforces the Führer principle in his movement.

At a meeting hall on the 4th November 1921 a battle between 800 Marxists and 46 National Socialists takes place. Hitler gives the order not to retreat. Afterwards he gives the hall guard the name "Sturmabteilung" (SA.). Adolf Hitler says: "Terror is broken by terror!"

When the internal disintegration and the external pressure of Germany's enemies comes to a climax in 1923, Adolf Hitler decides to take action. It comes to pass on 9 November 1923.

This uprising is crushed by treason. Adolf Hitler and many of his closest comrades-in-arms are arrested and the Hitler trial takes place.

Adolf Hitler is imprisoned for five years. In the Landsberg fortress he writes his book "Mein Kampf " , which contains his far-reaching ideological and political outlook

V. Re-establishment of the party and the struggle of Adolf Hitler's movement for power in Germany[5]

On December 19, 1924, Adolf Hitler was released from prison and immediately began to rebuild his movement. He begins his uncompromising struggle for Germany all over again.

1927 for the first time a party congress is held in Nuremberg. 12,000 activists were marching, sometimes including the columns of the ⚡⚡. Everywhere in the Reich, Adolf Hitler's movement is now increasingly asserting itself against all other parties.

The elections of 14. September 1930 represents the overwhelming breakthrough of the NSDAP. instead of the previous 12 seats in the Reichstag now it was 107 seats

Adolf Hitler moves to the centre of world political interests. Despite the prohibition and terror, the strong movement of the Führer can no longer be crushed.

1932 the last attempt by Marxism and the forces of reaction to prevent the Führer from taking over power.

The setback of 1932 only strengthens the inner strength of the Führer and his movement, everything that is lazy and weak falls away.

The Führer and his fellow fighters are called upon to meet the highest demands in terms of nerve and mental strength.

Political intrigues once again try to push the Führer onto a dead track.

The political momentum and energy of the movement, and above all the political genius of Adolf Hitler, overcome these last obstacles.

Adolf Hitler is the living example of the type of man who, coming from the broad masses of the people, succeeds in rising to the highest leadership position of his people through ability, energy and clear objectives.

On 30 January 1933, the aged Field Marshal Hindenburg entrusted Adolf Hitler with the Chancellorship of the Reich. This day marked the beginning of a genuine German revolution that encompassed all areas of human and national existence.

After the death of Hindenburg, Adolf Hitler became the bearer of the title supreme commander of the Reich.

His name has become the symbol of Germany, he is the leader who will one day assume the same mythical contours for the German people as the great heroic figures of the great German past.

Reference:

1) Curriculum p. 50—52: "Mein Kampf" p. 1—17.

2) Curriculum, pp. 52-55: "Mein Kampf", pp. 18-20, 40-42, 53-55, 59-65, 69-70.

3) Curriculum, pp. 55-57: "Mein Kampf", pp. 178-181, 250-310.

4) Curriculum, pp. 57-61: "The Path of the NSDAP", pp. 29-74; "Mein Kampf" pp. 400-402, 405-408,

5) Curriculum, pp. 61-65: "The Path of the NSDAP", pp. 75-142.

ϟϟ HANDBLÄTTER

FÜR DEN WELTANSCHAULICHEN UNTERRICHT

Lesson 7

Adolf Hitler fights for Germany

What did Adolf Hitler give to the German people ?

"National Socialism consciously places the people at the centre of all its thoughts and actions. "

Adolf Hitler

I. What did Adolf Hitler find when he came to power? [1]

After years of bitter hardship, mass misery and deepest humiliation, the Reich found itself in an extreme, year-round perilous situation.

Marxism prepared for bloody civil war.

The weak attitude of the previous governments in Germany made it easy for the communist to keep the whole of public life under terror.

Party squabbles and internal disputes fuelled the growing decline.

Class hatred and common conceit drove the inner cohesion of the German people ever further apart.

Unscrupulous party politics prepared for the disintegration of the Reich

With the erosion of all religious and religious foundations through racial and alien forces and ideas, the work of destroying the German national force had reached its climax.

Jewish greed destroyed all the high creative values of German culture, Judaism crept into all areas of German cultural life and, by dominating the press, radio, film, theatre and literature, destroyed all genuine German nationalism and thus prepared the spiritual and mental pre-conditions for its international goals.

In the economy and politics, the Jews were able to sneak into all decisive positions through unscrupulous methods and thus subjugated the German people

More than six million unemployed, ruined finances, a destroyed economy, a ruined peasantry were part of the terrible legacy that Adolf Hitler inherited.

In foreign policy terms, the Reich was defenceless. The 100,000-man army, with its poor technical equipment, would not even have been in a position to fully repel an attack by a small neighbouring state (no heavy weapons, no air force, etc.).

A system of military alliances held the Reich in its grip.

The Reich had become dishonourable because unscrupulous German politicians had acknowledged the Reich's war guilt in Versailles.

This was the legacy that Adolf Hitler took over on 30 January 1933.

II. Elimination of parliamentary system, party insurgency, destruction of Marxism, orientation of the Führer state and strong Reich power [2]

As a prerequisite for building the National Socialist Reich, Adolf Hitler removes the terror of the Marxist parties with a hard grip and smashes the parties.

In the place of an irresponsible parliamentary political system incapable of making real decisions, he establishes the Führer state.

The state no longer serves the special interests of individuals groups, royal houses or professions.

The National Socialist state, built on the natural foundations given by the people, is the highest form of the organized will of the community.

Compared to the liberalist "night-watchman state", the National Socialist state is, in the truest sense of the word, the official guardian of the nation.

The people's leadership is carried by the best, the boldest and most responsible men of the German people. The supreme decision-making body is not an irresponsible parliament, but the Führer.

The special rights of individual states are replaced by the overall interests of the Reich. An authoritative Reich law unites all the forces of the Reich in a unified way, creatively planning and leading.

III. Eliminating unemployment, building up the economy, creating a real national community and realising National Socialism [3]

In a very short time Adolf Hitler succeeds in eliminating unemployment; The slogan of the time of struggle "Work and bread for every German" is thus realised.

The right to work becomes the basis of the National Socialist state.

The entire economy is withdrawn from private capitalist interests and subordinated to the demands of the common good of the people.

The peasantry is being put back on a healthy foundation.

The law on the organization of national work removes the opposition between workers and employers and creates a community of leaders and followers. The core principle of the party program *"Community use goes before self-use"* finds its realisation through the creation of a real community of the people.

True Socialism

"We envision a state in which in the future every position should be filled by the most capable son of our people, regardless of where he comes from; a state in which birth is nothing and performance and ability is everything."

Adolf Hitler

"Honouring the work and the worker" is becoming an ethical principle of the working German people.

In place of charity and mercy, which is not obligatory, the Führer sets the obligation to stand up for the community with every sacrifice.

With the creation of the German Labour Front, all working German people are united in a large community of workers.

The expansion of social measures, such as housing construction, building new housing estates, social insurance, NS.-national welfare , occupational safety, KdF., Beauty of work, after-work and leisure activities, improves the life of working German people, their productivity is increased

A well-planned nationwide training programme (Reichsberufswettkampf) gives the strongest talents, regardless of birth and money, the opportunity to develop in the best possible way.

IV. Adolf Hitler's educational work on the German people [4]

In a tremendous educational work on the German people, Adolf Hitler ensures that the earlier Marxist and liberalist thinking disappears and the German people become more and more National Socialist in attitude and action.

Terms that were once laughed at, such as: honour, loyalty, faith, obedience, achievement, firmness of character, sacrifice, fulfilment of duty, freedom of the people, are being placed at the centre as the real focus of life.

In the HJ., BDM, in the Party, the branches, educational institutions such as NPEA., Adolf Hitler schools, Order Castles, in the labour service, in the Armed Forces, German people are formed according to National Socialist principles.

In this way Adolf Hitler ensures that National Socialism is not temporary, but remains the fundamental inner law of the German people for all time to come

V. Adolf Hitler as the creator of a strong cultural life [5]

Out of his great artistic genius, Adolf Hitler fertilized the entire cultural life of the German people, which was overgrown by foreign thinking.

Out of his mind, through his ideas, huge buildings emerge, which are the expression of a pure and strong artistic creator's will.

Architecture, music, painting, film, theatre and literature are once again connected to the people and thus an expression of a genuine cultural will that is appropriate to the Race.

Every person has a share in the cultural goods of the people.

VI. Adolf Hitler creates the conditions for the eternity of the German people [6]

Racial studies are made the basis for building up the German people and their state.

The doctrine of the equality of everything human is contrasted with the knowledge of the eternal value of the race.

The basic laws of heredity become essential elements of National Socialist leadership.

Measures created by the Führer: Law for the Prevention of Hereditarily Diseased Offspring, Law for the Preservation of Pure Blood, Law for the Protection of German Blood and German Honour,

Awakening the Will to the Family and to the Child, Fighting against the Decline in Births (Marriage Loans, Family Burden Equalisation), Mother and Child Relief Organisation, Settlement Activities, Promotion of Public Health through Health Management Measures

A strong, vigorous farmer as a source of life for the German folk is created by the Führer.

The German folk are once again bound to the soil

The security of food for the German people is created (battle of production)

VII. Adolf Hitler gives the German people their freedom to the outside world [7]

The four-year plans liberate Germany as far as possible from its dependence on foreign countries in the field of raw material procurement.

The economy of the German people is becoming independent of the world.

Adolf Hitler restores freedom in foreign policy and the honour of the German people by leaving the League of Nations (October 14th, 1933).

On March 16, 1935, the Führer restores Germany's military sovereignty with the reintroduction of national military conscription.

Strong Armed Forces protect the Reich.

In January 1935, the Saar region is returned to the Reich.

In March 1936, the entry of the new National Socialist Armed Forces took place in the Rhineland.

On January 30th, 1937, the Führer solemnly withdraws his signature from the Versailles dictate of shame.

On March 12, 1938, the Führer was able to announce to history *"the greatest accomplishment of his life":* his homeland, Austria, has returned home

With this, the National Socialist Greater German Reich, the longing of a millennium of German history, has become reality. In October 1938, the Sudetenland also returns home.

On 14th March 1939, Slovakia, which had become independent, placed its fate into the hands of the Führer.

On March 16th, Bohemia and Moravia again become a sphere of influence for the Reich

On March 21st, 1939, Lithuania returned Memel to Germany. *"One people, One Nation, One Führer"* becomes reality.

This is how Adolf Hitler built Greater Germany in six years of tireless, hard work for peace. The shame and disgrace of 9 November 1918 was thus erased.

This purposeful, peaceful work of building up a new greatness for the Reich was abruptly interrupted by the fury and the intent of destruction of the opponents of a strong racial power and a united, organised Europe: the capitalist powers of England and America and Bolshevism and the power of Judaism which dominated them all.

On 1st September 1939, war broke out which, in its wake, brought about a fundamental change in the way the world was viewed.

On September 2 and 3, 1939, Britain and France declared war on Germany after Adolf Hitler had repeatedly made practical suggestions for maintaining peace, especially vis-à-vis Britain. Churchill had already said in 1936: *"Germany is becoming too strong; it must be destroyed."*

Reference:

1) The way of the NSDAP. Pp. 15-28; 48. — X42. Curriculum p. 65. Pocket calendar 1544 p. 45.

2-7) Curriculum, pp. 65-70; Pp. 71-88. Pocket calendar 1944 pp. 47-54

Lesson 8

National Socialism saves the Nordic Germanic heritage of Europe

"Germany is called to liberate all the cultivated peoples of the continent, not by trying to impose its own peculiarity on foreign peoples, but by pointing each nation to itself and its own special history".

The Danish writer Steffens

Europe is a creation of Nordic mankind

Europe was created by the Nordic spirit, will and strength. The cultures of Greece and Rome became great through the creative power of Nordic mankind.

They disintegrated when the Nordic blood of the ruling class was weakened by mixing with inferior races and degeneration. The Viking campaigns stretched across Europe; in Russia too they founded Germanic empires.

The common culture is the basis of Europe's inner unity

In spite of their different geographical locations, traditions and living conditions, the individual European nations have a common culture. Every nation has its system of governance and its way of life, but the great men and their ideas belong to all of Europe e.g., Martin Luther, Beethoven, Mozart, Goethe, Kant, Nietzsche, Molière, Rembrandt, Rubens, Goya, Michelangelo, Leonardo da Vinci, Shakespeare, Houston Stuart Chamberlain, Henrik Ibsen, Grieg, Sven Hedin, Knut Hamsun.

45

These values are fought for with common sacrifices, e.g.. the fight against the Moors in Spain and France, against the onslaught of the Mongols and Huns from the east, against Rome in the Thirty Years War.

Hellas, Rome and Germanism - the historical bearers of the European task

Europe was first embodied by the odorous country, then by Rome, then by the Germaen (German-Roman Empire).

The northern countries were united in the Kalmar Union under Margaret of Sweden. However, this union did not last long. The farmers revolted because the Central European aristocrats who were appointed did not take into account the different national characteristics of the Nordic peoples. The north was a great power at the time, ruled the Baltic Sea region, Finland and the Baltic states.

Europe's fragmentation, Catholic Church and Counter-Reformation

(Huguenots)

Pressure from the East - the Greek Catholic Church in the service of Russian imperialism - Peter I. Last but not least, the British Sea and the French Revolution, fuelled by Jews and Freemasons, have the leadership of the Nordic countries People destroyed and put in their place the rule of money and the mob.

Capitalism and supranational powers used Jewish methods such as lies and deceit to fight the leading Nordic spirit. The Norse man and warrior, who loved battle and freedom, perished in this atmosphere or fled from the land. The Nordic man, whose free personality and whose creative urge could no longer develop, had to go into the world as a pioneer. Streams of the best Nordic blood went to America, to the overseas colonies and to the big cities.

Germanism as a champion of Europe

Germanism, hardened by many struggles, as the centre of power against all fragmentation, has always held Europe together. In order to eliminate and destroy this power, the Jews and the Britain they ruled incited for war.

German National Socialism led the rebirth of the Continent

Of all the countries in Europe, Germany suffered the most from the Versailles pseudo-peace. In the greatest need, Adolf Hitler became a liberator and created the German-Nordic way of life in stark contrast to Jewish materialism, monetary rule and democratic mass doctrine..

The strongest powers in the world are belief and ideology, if they are realistic, correct and connected to the laws of nature

National Socialism as a Nordic Worldview

Because the Führer's thoughts were correct, National Socialism has become more than just German politics - it has become the new Nordic worldview. The Führer's struggle and ideas were understood and embraced far beyond the borders.

Adolf Hitler, the liberator of Europe

The front soldier Adolf Hitler comes from the depths of the people. He felt the weight of a historical destiny on his shoulders. He saw that the bourgeoisie was no longer fulfilling its tasks as a preserving and creative element. Through him the seemingly impossible was made possible. He woke the desperate and freedom-loving from dull inaction and called on all creative forces to fight against the world enemy.

The Führer has built a better community. In doing so he gave the Nordic man with a healthy instinct again a sense of security and life again. And not only in Germany, also in Europe and around the world. National Socialism thus becomes a Nordic worldview that fertilizes all creative and fighting elements.

In this way, a new culture and the "Germanic age" is brought up. Proof of this are the volunteers from all countries who are fighting in our ranks.

The National Socialist organisation in the Germanic Countries

Throughout Europe, organisations similar to those of the NSDAP were established. created by men who also strove for liberation from Judaism. Since 1933 the Jews have left no stone unturned to prevent the formation of such organizations in other countries. Encircling Germany.

At the end of the war there will be the victory of the political soldier of National Socialism

The fight against National Socialism is being waged by the enemy with all weapons. Any means will do for the enemy. The small and neutral states are threatened and exposed to bomb terror; in the areas occupied by German troops, illegal propaganda of lies is being used and hounded from this side.

And yet political soldiers are coming from all countries to take up arms, men who are voluntarily fighting against the world enemy. We must all be political soldiers in this struggle between our National Socialist world and the Jewish world.

All the countries of Europe will stand or fall with the victory of Germany.

SS

HANDBLÄTTER
FÜR DEN WELTANSCHAULICHEN UNTERRICHT

Lesson 9

Only a strong Reich saves Europe

Part I

The Reich is our obligation

"When one speaks of the 'Reich', whether in America, in Asia, in Russia, in Japan, then only one Reich is meant, this Germanic Reich of the German Nation."

Heinrich Himmler

I. The Reich is as old as the German people themselves. It embodies the historical mission of the nation.[1]

The Germanic peoples laid the foundation for what was to become Europe.

The Frankish Empire as the forerunner of the formation of the German Empire. Carl the Great, the creator of the Germanic West and unifier of the German tribes.

The founding of the empire and the development of the people under Henry I: Germanic rule and Germanic nationhood in the Middle Ages.

II. The Reich of the Middle Ages - the dress rehearsal of the German people in the leadership of the West. [2]

Otto the Great becomes Emperor and leader of the Germanic West. The German people become the enforcers of the European constitution of the Reich:

49

Protection and shielding of the West against the Avars, Saracens, Magyars, Mongols, Turks and wielder of a just order within.

Highlights of medieval imperial history - Saxons, Salians and Hohenstaufen: Henry I (unification, victory in Hungary, founding of cities); Otto the Great (emperorship, annexation of Italy, colonisation of the East); Conrad II and Henry III (annexation of Bohemia, annexation of Italy, colonisation of the East). (annexation of Bohemia, Burgundy, Hungary and Poland); Frederick I Barbarossa (the legend of the emperor in the mountains); Henry VI (Italy, half of France, Britain, North Africa, Cyprus and Armenia dependent on the empire).

The old Reich perished neither from military defeats nor from racial disintegration: it was brought down by the power-hungry Papacy, which knew how to make skilful use of German discord (Henry IV, Gregory VII and Canossa).

III. German   forces continue the European task after the collapse of the Kaiser Reich[3]

The greatest work of colonisation in European history: the German eastward expansion.

It is initiated by the Saxon rulers (Henry I, Otto the Great), continued by Henry the Lion and crowned by the Teutonic Order and the Hanseatic League.

The Teutonic Order: Embodiment of the Germanic idea of allegiance, nucleus of the Prussian state (concept of "serving").

Conquest and settlement of the Baltic region.

Reasons for disintegration: Too few peasants. No offspring.

The Hanseatic League of cities anchored in Germany from Flanders to Norway and Estonia.

In the field of trade policy, it fulfils a task which by right should have fallen to a strong empire. The "Royal Merchant".

IV.(Briefly touched on)

The failure of an imperial power to regulate the European civil wars. - Attempts at order from the inevitably failure.[4]

Spain's attempt to organise Europe from the south-west corner in alliance with the Roman Church fails due to the resistance of Germanic Lutheranism (Geuse, North German princes), Britain and France.

France's attempt to dominate Europe militarily (Louis XIV, Napoleon) fails because it is unable to overcome the German centre of the continent (Prince Eugene, Frederick the Great, Stein, Scharnhorst) and because of Britain's resistance.

Since its rise to maritime power, Britain has been concerned only with maintaining European discord ("European equilibrium") in order to have its back free for its policy of plunder throughout the world.

Its tactic: fight the strongest power on the continent by uniting the many smaller ones.

Britain's policy: with France and Holland against Spain, with Spain and France against Holland, with Spain, Holland and others against France, with France and all others against Germany.

Europe as a whole stands and falls with the presence of a strong Reich. It is clear from history that the heyday of the Reich coincides with the periods of Europe's powerful influence in the world and the prosperous cooperation of its peoples among themselves. Europe and the Reich are fatefully intertwined, and one is inconceivable in the long run without the other.

Reference :

1) Der Weg zum Reich, pp. 30-47; Das Reich und Europa, pp. 2-11; Lehrplan f. d. weltansch. Education, pp. 25-30

2) W. z. R., pp. 48-52; R. u. E., pp. 11-21; Lehrpl., pp. 29-33

3) W. z. R., pp. 52-60; R. u. E., pp. 21-23; Lehrpl., pp. 33-35

4) R. u. E., pp. 25-32; syllabus, pp. 35-39

SS HANDBLÄTTER
FÜR DEN WELTANSCHAULICHEN UNTERRICHT

Lesson 10

Only a strong Reich saves Europe

Part II

With the Reich the European community arises anew

"We know that we stand in the decisive hour of German history, but we also know that never before have the flags of the Reich been carried forward more consciously and with a harder hand, and that no power in the world is any longer able to prevent this rebirth of Germany and the Reich for the salvation of Europe."

Alfred Rosenberg

I. Peasants' War, Religious Struggle and 30 Years' War: The Low Point of Imperial Power and the Completion of European Anarchy.[1]

The attempts of the peripheral nations to organise themselves had to fail, because the continent could only be organised from Central Europe.

Germany is destined to lead the continent for reasons of a) its geopolitical position, b) its numerical superiority, c) its blood composition, d) its state order (Reich as a supranational form of existence).

In the best Germans, the desire for a strong Reich was always awake: peasant and knight uprisings, Ulrich von Hutten. Luther as the champion of German intellectual freedom (distorted by his heirs).

Only a strong Reich guarantees the existence of the German people and the continental order: the Thirty Years' War, a European fratricidal war of the greatest magnitude, is fought on the back of a powerless Germany. (Out of 20 million Germans, about 11 million perish).

A new great danger from the East: the Turks. The Ostmark (Austria) of the fragmented Reich is the last protective wall of the continent.

II. Re-emergence of the German centre of Europe. The two centres of power on new colonial territory: Austria and Prussia.[2]

Austria grows in its defensive struggle against the Turks. Imperial Field Marshal Prince Eugen: too protective to the west and south, too powerful to the south-east. The Danube region is opened up to German power and culture.

Prussia, which also emerged from the border struggle, became the nucleus of a new formation of the Reich. The Great Elector and the Soldier-King form the foundations of the Prussian state: officer corps and civil service.   Highest values: honour, loyalty and duty.

Frederick the Great, the founder of Prussia's position of great power and creator of the Prussian idea of the state.

The Frederician example: a precondition for the spiritual rebirth of Germany.

Unification of Germany and re-foundation of the Reich in the 19th century through the Prussian-Austrian conflict (Silesian Wars, Seven Years' War).

Collapse of the outdated Prussian state structure before Napoleon. Rise of Prussia under Stein - Scharnhorst - Gneisenau.

The wars of liberation: a flare-up of the German will for unity and empire.

The painful struggle of the German people to find a political form that suits them in the 19th century: Fraternities, Revolution

Growing tension in Europe; the tyranny of Britain, the unfruitful imperialism of France, the threatening interference of Russia.

III. Bismarck re-founds the Reich and establishes a European peace system under German leadership.[3]

Bismarck shapes Prussia into an instrument of German unification. Bismarck's peace emerges in three wars: 1864 (with Denmark), 1866 (with Austria), 1870-71 (with France).

Bismarck's domestic policy: federal state, tight military and economic policy, the most advanced workers' legislation in the world.

Bismarck's foreign (European) vision: European peace system, based on a balance of interests from the centre. Bismarck the "coachman of Europe" (Berlin Congress).

The enemies of the Bismarck Reich: clerics, freemasons and Marxists. Cultural struggle and socialist law.

IV. The loss of the First World War was the fault of Germany's political leadership at the time.[4]

Wilhelm II, the small heir to a great legacy. Germany had already lost the First World War politically - internally and externally - while it was still militarily undefeated.

Versailles: The second great low point in German history.

The movement of the Führer renews the popular power of the Germans and lays the foundation for the re-establishment of a German west Reich out of a National Socialist spirit. By 1939, Adolf Hitler had laid the foundations for a more just order on the European continent and created the conditions for the coming struggle for European freedom: the elimination of the Bolshevik outpost in Spain, the establishment of the protectorate, the pacification of the south-east.

The Second World War: continuation and conclusion of a thirty-year struggle for the Reich and its order. Clear fronts.

The Reich is the bearer of the struggle for Europe and the shaper of the future order of the united Europe. The New Order of the continent, both politically and socially, will be under the aegis of a revolutionary European socialism. It is up to each nation to determine its own position within the continental community, on the basis of its contribution to the whole.

In the Reich, the great and sorrowful history of the West finds its final fulfilment.

Reference :

1) Der Weg zum Reich, pp. 64-76, Das Reich und Europa, pp. 31-36, Lehrplan f. d. weltansch.

Education, pp. 37-39.

2) W. z. R., pp. 76-91; R. u. E., pp. 36-44; Lehrplan., pp. 41-4;.

3) W. z. R., pp. 91-96; R. u. E., pp. 44-46; Lehrplan., pp. 45-46.

4) W. z. R., pp. 104-115; R. u. E., pp. 46-48; Lehrplan., pp. 46-47.

SS HANDBLÄTTER
FÜR DEN WELTANSCHAULICHEN UNTERRICHT

Lesson 11

Reich and Europe in danger !

Outline:

I. The position of Europe among the world powers

1. New Great Powers:

The globe is undergoing the formation of new, formidable power clusters.

a) The USA today dominates not only the northern half of the entire American continent, including Canada and Mexico, but also, through the power of the dollar, the South American states. On the western hemisphere of the earth, a continent is forming that is politically and economically led by the Jewry of New York. The mineral resources, the fertility of the earth, the extension through all the climates of the earth and the enormous expansion of the spaces allow the emergence here of a power such as the earth has never known before in such great masses.

b) The Soviet Union dominates the north of Asia and the east of Europe. Vast areas from Moscow to Vladivostok also contain enormous riches of fertile soil, mineral resources and raw materials. The aim of the Soviets, in continuation of Tsarist imperialism, is access to warm seas: Atlantic, Mediterranean, Indian Ocean.

c) In the Far East, under the leadership of our Japanese ally, the new "Greater East Asia" is emerging, which also represents a concentration of power of continental proportions.

2. European small nations and states:

Europe comprises over 30 nations, the majority of which have between 2 and 8 million inhabitants. From the perspective of the previously mentioned metropolitan states, the European peoples and states appear very small. The relationship of these small peoples to the new metropolitan states is similar to the relationship of the small German states around 1800 to today's Greater Germany.

The earth is under the law of new, great concentrations of power, made possible by the advances of technology in communications, transport, economics and warfare.

Can these small peoples and states of Europe maintain themselves in today's situation of world politics?

II. The adversaries of Europe

1. Bolshevism

The rulers of the Moscow Kremlin want to dominate the world. They are pursuing their goal in stages.

In 1935, the then Soviet ambassador in Paris, Potemkin, told the then Minister of War, Fabry: *"Out of the world war came the Russia of the Soviets, out of the next war will come the Europe of the Soviets."* A Soviet officer recently captured in the East openly declares, *"If we succeed in eliminating Germany, we will start the war against Britain. - There will be only two ruling powers of the future world, each in its own hemisphere: America and Soviet Russia. Britain would only create intrigue, therefore we will destroy her."*

And in the summer of 1938, the President of the Soviet Union, Kalinin, writes: *"The victory of Bolshevism in the Soviet Union must be considered incomplete as long as the other states of the world still have a form of government different from the Bolshevik regime."*

Here is pronounced as the goal the Bolshevisation of all mankind, including the American hemisphere.

The Swedish scholar Sven Hedin writes in these days: *"If the Soviet plan succeeds, a Bolshevisation of fantastic proportions awaits us. Although the population of Europe is twice as great as that of Russia, its high culture will not give its stamp to the crude and primitive Russian masses, but on the contrary it will be dragged down to the low level of the conquering race. The watchword will be innumerable mass graves and deportations to immense Siberia. In order that the Bolshevik regime may live, Western culture must be exterminated."*

2. Britain

Britain brought about this war in order to maintain its European supremacy. It supported the small state of Poland in its challenging behaviour towards Germany, in order not to support it afterwards either in war or politically. Britain's betrayal of Poland will not be forgotten by any country in Europe.

Today Britain is struggling to retain some remnants of its former world empire. The sell-out of the Empire is in full swing. The South African Prime Minister Smuts declared some time ago that Britain would be incomparably poorer after this war than before it. So Britain has already lost her war.

Sven Hedin writes: *"Within a Bolshevised Europe it will not be long before Britain is an easy prey. The disgusting thing about this spectacle is that two nations standing at the height of Western education are sacrificing the utmost of their strength in material and human resources to destroy a continent which is the original home and stronghold of our culture. The sickness and madness of this war lies in the blind frenzy with which the Western powers are working for its downfall."*

"If they succeed in crushing Germany, the way will be open for the advance of the frontiers of the Soviet Russian Republic to the Baltic, the Mediterranean, the Channel, the Atlantic."

3. Americanism

The world domination aspirations of the dollar imperialists of New York and Washington are the driving reason for the involvement of the U.S. in this war. So far the New York Jews have done excellent business. Not only have they achieved the closer union of Canada with the U.S., not only have they eliminated the weak resistance of the South American states to the domination of Washington, they have also gained a foothold east of the Atlantic, in West Africa, North Africa, Ireland, Britain and Iceland, and are not willing to vacate these "bridgeheads" later.

What America brings us becomes clear in southern Italy: plundering of cultural treasures, starvation of the population, defenceless abandonment of women to the white and coloured mercenary troops, criminality, insecurity, epidemics. The Americans would only plunder a Europe they had conquered, deport or starve the population, but would not do anything to rebuild it.

4. World Freemasonry

One of the secret world powers which has not only brought about the amalgamation of many moneyed interests to form the gigantic edifice of modern world capitalism, but also seeks by criminal means to undermine every healthy popular force, to eliminate powerful leaders and to spread the spirit of decomposition, is World Freemasonry. Its ultimate leadership is clearly in Jewish hands.

5 World Jewry

The driving force of American dollar imperialism is Judaism. President Roosevelt, who himself has Jewish blood, has surrounded himself with Jews as his closest advisers and has only to carry out the orders of his secret commissioners.

The same Jewry has succeeded in getting the key positions of the Soviet economy into its hands. Thus the Soviet Union today is a strange mixture of state capitalism and private usury. But both paths, state capitalism and private capitalism, lead to the same goal in the Soviet Union: the domination of Jewry.

What Europe has to expect from a world domination of Jewry has become so clear in the Baltic states temporarily occupied by the Red troops, in White Russia, the Ukraine and Bessarabia, as well as in Southern Italy and North Africa, that no people with awake senses can have the slightest doubt.

III. Europe's options

Europe is faced with the choice: either the destruction of all independent nationality, all freedom and justice, all culture-creating people and sinking into slavery and barbarism - or the uniting of all forces for common defence and common security.

Sven Hedin writes: "*Through the conferences in Moscow, Cairo and Teheran, Stalin has been certified that Britain and America are not putting any obstacles in the way of his advance towards the Atlantic. Britain and America have handed over the fate of Europe to Bolshevism.*"

In the face of this development there is only one salvation: the unification of the European family of nations under the leadership of the Reich.

Sven Hedin writes: "Germany is the only power capable of saving not only Europe but mankind from the greatest misfortune, the most terrible disgrace that has ever existed".

IV. The Reich defends Europe

The Reich not only takes on the military protection of Europe against the onrushing Bolshevism and the threat of Americanism. It also defends European culture. Adolf Hitler's Germany fights for

1. Social justice

Only the folkish socialism of Adolf Hitler strives for the genuine welfare of working people and realises social justice. In both Capitalist and Bolshevik countries the worker finds only exploitation and lack of rights.

2. A free peasantry

A down-to-earth, strong peasantry is the root of all national culture. Only in Europe is there still a healthy peasantry.

Adolf Hitler: *"The German people will either be a peasant people or it will not be."*

3. Languages and Peoples:

Europe's wealth of peoples, cultural languages and folk traditions is unsurpassed. Every nation rightly sees the cultivation of its own language, its native folklore, as the most important cultural task and the root of its national existence. In the European family of nations, each nation will be able to remain true to its own language and culture, its own national character and folklore, and will be able to make its own contribution to the overall development of Europe.

4. Freedom and Independence

Neither in Bolshevik centralism nor in the cultureless spirit of dollar imperialism is there real freedom and independence for the small peoples. Only a political idea which starts from the primordial reasons of life and wants to obey the eternal laws of life, which therefore thinks of the welfare of the people and not of its own power and advantage, can therefore preserve the freedom and independence of the small peoples.

Poland demonstrates with all desirable clarity what our opponents have in mind for the small peoples.

5 Culture

Bolshevism and Americanism feed on European culture. They have created nothing of their own in the cultural field. They will prevent any freedom of creative development, place every cultural creation in the service of their striving for power and thus degrade it. Culture must grow.

None of the leading men of the present day has more understanding for the creative forces of the peoples than Adolf Hitler. Leon Degrelle, the leader of the Wallon people, said of the Führer on 20th April 1944:

"The astonishing statesman who holds in his strong hands twenty European peoples, the warrior with the unexpected reactions or that long patience which is even more beautiful than the lightning-like actions of the people. More beautiful than the lightning-like actions, is also an astonishing poet and has a heart wide open to the emotions of the humblest souls. By the way, poets alone can change the world, for they alone possess that freshness and that ardour which make them overcome all difficulties, they alone throw on reality that light which makes everything more beautiful, warmer and brighter."

V. The European family of nations

The leadership of Europe, according to its situation and strength, can only be assumed by the Reich. The Swede Sven Hedin said:

"The Germans are the most capable of all peoples; that is why they are to be put down by the Bolshevists. As engineers, merchants and colonisers, the Germans are more successful than other peoples; that is why Britain and America want to destroy their factories and trading cities. The German soldiers are the best in the world, that is why they should be defeated and disarmed with the help of Russia."

Only a victorious Reich can give the threatened Europe the firm support and the strong centre it needs.

The European family of peoples is rallying around this Reich in peaceful cooperation. Europe's peoples know that a social transformation will be the greatest event of the post-war period

"The socialist revolution will arise from the blood of the front. The Führer wants it. He is preparing it. He is doing everything to accelerate it. We know that the aim of his struggle is to bring justice, prosperity and respect to the worker. The soldier who fights and suffers does so without complaining because this radiant hope sustains him. The war is only a stage to be overcome as soon as possible. Behind the war lies the mighty and peaceful revolt which will make of Europe, torn asunder yesterday, a great socialist community."

Léon Degrelle

ᛋᛋ HANDBLÄTTER

FÜR DEN WELTANSCHAULICHEN UNTERRICHT

Lesson 12

EUROPE'S DEADLY ENEMY – Bolshevism !

"We must have no doubt that at this time the fate of Europe for the next thousand years will be decided."

Adolf Hitler on 8 November 1941

I. What is Europe?

Shaped for millennia by the power of Nordic Indo-European peoples, Europe, for all the diversity of its ethnic, cultural and political make-up, is nevertheless a unity and is always striving anew towards unity.

The common basis of life of its peoples is related blood. For despite today's racial differences, Indo-Europeanism laid the foundation of cultural and political development for the whole of Europe, and Germany renewed and expanded this foundation.

Since the struggle of the Greeks against the Persians as masters of Asia, the idea of freedom has become the guiding principle of European development. This idea also lies in the high valuation of the personality, the creative achievement of the individual in the free community of people and state. Finally, the foundations for the unique intellectual development of Europe were laid in ancient Greece: the free search for truth, the unlimited will for ultimate knowledge, the development of a science that was neither limited nor inhibited by any priestly power. Ancient Rome attempted for the first time to unite a large part of Europe on a political basis and created further building blocks in state leadership and legal order; its world empire, however, perished in the Orientalisation. Since then, for 1500 years, the Germanic peoples have taken over and extended the inheritance of the Greeks and Romans: the preservation of human freedom, cultural wealth and state order. In addition, however, they created the Reich's idea and realised it for the first time in the Middle Ages, a new principle of order that preserved the higher unity of Europe above the wealth of its peoples and cultures and protected it from all enemies.

At the same time, Germanicism, led by the Germans, gave Europe its present-day face in centuries of intellectual struggle and renewed, expanded and preserved the cultural basis of the non-Germanic peoples as well. The belief in a divine world order, independent of the different denominations of its peoples, the idealism of thought, the sanctity of property, unite all peoples of Europe today with its Germanic core.

60

Thus, in spite of repeated fratricidal wars, in spite of centuries of internal tensions, Europe is still a unity in the fundamentals of culture, human attitudes, the legal system and the economy. Today, however, it is striving for a stronger concentration of its unity in order to preserve its existence from the threat from the East and the West and to win a new, better future.

Europe is for all of us a community of nations, the gateway to culture and human dignity.

II. Why is Bolshevism the mortal enemy of Europe?

The origin of Bolshevism is the world domination idea of Judaism and the Asiatic despotism of Ghengis Khan: both united in its founder, the half-breed Lenin, also by blood.

Its spiritual basis, Marxism, is pure materialism and denies religion, higher culture, human dignity and property, wants to exterminate all peoples and instead establish a world proletariat which no longer knows any differences of race, culture and social gradation.

The essence of Bolshevism., as it has already been carried out in Russia is the annihilation of man as a higher being in general.

Its aim is: the extermination of the ruling class which has grown out of race and people, the elimination of all meaningful ethnic divisions, the abolition of private property, the indiscriminate proletarianisation of all countries and peoples. As in Russia, also in Europe a coercive state is to be erected on the completely disenfranchised, will-less and soulless human masses, which would be the last foundation for the final conquest of world domination.

Russia, where Bolshevism was first able to carry out its diabolical experiment on men and peoples, had for decades been accustomed to a despotic system through Mongol rule and Tsarism. Political or human freedom has never played a role in Russia.

Europe has lived from the idea of freedom since its beginnings. Never has a violent state been able to exist in Europe for a longer period of time.

Bolshevism has enslaved all the peoples of its huge empire even more than Tsarism before it - it has wiped out every conscious people with their own culture and way of life.

Europe lives from the diversity of its peoples - even small nationalities shaped their own culture and administration.

In Bolshevik Russia, private property has been almost completely eliminated with the destruction of small-scale farming. The peoples of Europe can only preserve their rich culture and civilisation, their technical and social achievements, their high standard of living on the basis of private property. The sanctity of property is a European principle.

In Russia, Bolshevism has degraded man from a higher living being to a proletarian, to a soulless state slave.

The European, living from the idea of freedom, can in the long run serve the state only in voluntary subordination; from this arises his creative achievement.

III. What follows from this?

The subjugation of Europe by Bolshevism would not only mean the political and military subjugation of its peoples. Bolshevism must destroy Europe, i.e., its races and people, if it is to establish its system here.

God-denying Marxism, it's purely materialistic conception of life, the annihilation of human dignity, the extinction of all freedom par excellence - every single one of these programme points means the death, the downfall of Europe.

The European cannot breathe in the air of the Bolshevik state dungeon; he needs freedom like he needs his daily bread. The German worker, after whom the working class of the whole of Europe is now orientated, is a creative man of labour with the will for a cultivated life and the right to own property. He would perish if German-European socialism were to succumb to Jewish-Asian Bolshevism.

There is only one salvation from the worst threat to its life known to Europe's two and a half thousand years of history: the renewal of its unity by the Reich as the leading power. "*If Europe is to exist as a whole, it needs leadership. A Europe without leadership would be a motionless lump, a Europe without leadership would fall apart at the first test of strength*". (Kleo Pleyer)

"*A pitiless and merciless war has been forced upon us by eternal Judaism, which, if it were not able to stop the elements of destruction before the borders of Europe, would turn this continent into a single field of ruins. But it would not be the burnt cities, the destroyed cultural monuments that would then remain as the worst consequence of this struggle, but the bestially slaughtered masses of people who would fall victim to this inner-Asian flood just as it had once been the case in the time of the Hun and Mongol storms.*"

Adolf Hitler

Reference :

1) Europe and Bolshevism

2) Fighting Bolshevism

SS HANDBLÄTTER
FÜR DEN WELTANSCHAULICHEN UNTERRICHT

Lesson 13

This is Bolshevism!

We know the theoretical principle and the cruel truth of the aims of this world plague. It is called the rule of the proletariat and it is the dictatorship of Jewry! In Russian Bolshevism we have to see the attempt of Judaism, undertaken in the 20th century, to take over world domination.

Adolf Hitler

I. Origin of Bolshevism

Founded by the Jewish-Tatarian half-breed Lenin, Bolshevism is the political system that seeks to bring into reality the teachings of the Jew Karl Marx, Marxism or Communism.

II. Main slogans of Marxism

Man and human "society" are products of matter; family, race and people only artificial products. Denial of any divine world order, of all spiritual, moral and emotional values. Denial of property. Demand: Establishment of the International, the classless society of all people through world revolution: *"Proletarians of all countries unite!"*

The main goal, kept secret from the peoples, is Jewish world domination after the destruction of all peoples, states and cultures by the chaos of the world revolution.

III. Path of the Bolshevik Revolution

The starting point of Bolshevism in Russia, where the most favourable preconditions are present: a primitive, immensely suffering mass of people, decomposition of the leading strata in the tsarist system, social misery of the industrial workers and the land-hungry small peasantry, in addition to terrible blood losses through the war.

63

The victory of Bolshevism brought about by a small, tightly disciplined organization with dictatorial leadership by Lenin and powerful proclamations: Total socialization of industry! All land to the peasants!

- Years of struggle to secure power at home. The Cheka, to which millions of innocent people fell victim, ensured the purposeful suppression of any resistance with a sophisticated terror system. In addition, from the beginning rigorous propaganda and education methods. The industrial workers are fanatised by the belief in the future paradise of all working people.

Abroad, meanwhile, attempts to bring about communist revolution through the Comintern, the Communist International, with its headquarters in Moscow. In contrast to Trotsky and his friends, Stalin recognized that world revolution could not be achieved by internal decomposition alone. Therefore, since 1929, the new dictator chose a different path: the temporary concentration on Russia.

With the five-year plans Stalin tried to achieve the full implementation of the Bolshevik experiment in Russia. His goal:

(a) transformation of all people into proletarians. Thereby

b) Forming man into a will-less workhorse for the

c) Industrialisation of the entire economy, including agriculture. Thereby shall be achieved:

(d) The most enormous war production of all times.

Final goal:

(e) The Bolshevik world revolution through a new world war.

IV. The Methods

After the destruction of the main part of the former leadership and intelligence class, the Jews take their place everywhere. They also take over the shaping of the new type of man for the Bolshevik system. Only the uprooted Jew is able to carry out the transformation of the Russian, peasant-destined man into a soulless workhorse.

Propaganda and mass education expanded on a grand scale. Mental standardization by Marxism by all means. Limitation of instruction and specialised training to very specific areas. Everything directed toward industrialisation. Above all, the growing generation was to be political fanatics fanatisation and one-sided materialistic education in the "*new style of the Soviet man*".

From infancy on, shaping of man by Bolshevism; marriage, formerly sanctified by religion and sentiment, now merely procreative and childbearing mechanism. "Equal rights" of the woman in being brought up to any male activity, therefore rearing of the child in Bolshevik kindergartens and community schools. By hermetically closing off from any real European spiritual education, from the culture and life-world of other peoples, easy fanatisation of this youth, which grows up believing that it belongs to the most progressive social state on earth and that it will work and fight for the human paradise of the future.

Continuation and further expansion of terror complements the spiritual massification. The most radical effect, however, is the forcible conversion of all occupational groups and classes into proletarians. Since the first Five-Year Plan, the process of transformation has begun systematically: construction of huge industrial plants on the one hand - ruthless destruction of the peasantry on the other. The collective system expropriates countless millions of former peasants and displaces them as propertyless slaves to the new industrial centres or to forced labour camps. Millions of others perish of hunger, the rest remain as rural industrial workers on the kolkhoz and sovkhoz farms.

The goal of collectivisation, in Stalin's own words, was "*the equalisation of town and country,*" the multiplication of the industrial proletariat as the basis of "socialism." For the Bolshevist, agriculture is also "industry", consequently the peasants must also become proletarians.

The success: In 1939, according to the Soviet official statistics, only a residue of 1.8 percent of the total population with small peasant individual property still exists. - All the rest are dependent, propertyless workers and employees in town and country: proletarians. The entire economy of the Soviet Union is armament, every kind of industry only armament industry. Already ten years before the outbreak of the war, the Russian population, the labour slaves in town and country, were standardized to the lowest standard of living, just as today's Russian conscript receives in the war clothes, footwear, food and lodging only so much that service as a "soldier of the world revolution" is possible. - Millions work almost without pay in concentration and punishment camps of all kinds until they die, far worse off in clothing and food than Negro slaves of earlier centuries.

The success of this system (even before the war, according to a conservative estimate, 30 million dead) is obvious. The Jew has created a uniform mass of work animals in the largest body of states on earth. With them it was possible to build up an armament production which even today provides huge quantities of tanks, aeroplanes, guns and weapons of all kinds for the fight against the free peoples. These people, disenchanted, but intellectually fanatised by a false doctrine that has been ingrained for decades, and today still dominated by a mendaciously propagated "Patriotism", are also the best material for the giant battles in the East, nameless victims for the secret aims of world Jewry.

The danger of this system is enormous because of its purposeful execution. Lenin's words about the aims of Bolshevism are written today in huge letters behind the flags of the Red Army, which is supposedly fighting for the defence of its homeland: "Our aim is unalterably the attainment of world domination.... The rule of the Soviets knows neither freedom nor justice. This rule is based on suppression and negation of every individualistic will.... Ruthlessness to the extreme is our duty.... By complete tyranny - in the service of which is even every betrayal, every breach of word, even denial of the slightest shadow of justice - we shall press mankind down to the ultimate level of equality, which alone makes men fit to become the easily handled, uniform tools of our power."

For Germany and Europe, however, Adolf Hitler's insight applies with all its consequences:

"We Germans have only everything to gain in this struggle for being or not being. For the loss of this war would be our end anyway. Inner-Asian barbarism would come over Europe as in the times of the Huns or Mongols. No one knows this better than the German soldier and the nations allied with him, who learned at the front the essence of the Bolshevik liberation of mankind."

References

1) **Europe and Bolshevism**

2) **Fighting Bolshevism**

Lesson 14

A People's order of life against Bolshevik massification

How Bolshevism and National Socialism differ

I. How the German Soldier Experienced the Soviet Union

When the German worker crossed the borders of the Soviet Union as a soldier in 1941, he entered a new world. What he had heard, some thought to a large extent, was political propaganda. Memories of the Marxist slogans of the system era, which had been "forbidden" since 1933, lived on in some people. But from the first hour of the personal eye, everyone was converted. For where there was order in the homeland, here he saw only disorder and chaos. Where he had known self-evident cleanliness, here he saw only dirt. Where he had known decent clothing, here he saw rags. These were only small appearances. But the soldier is used to seeing everything from a practical point of view. A system that does not want to give him what the National Socialist worker regards as the minimum prerequisite for a contented life, namely a decent, orderly existence with the possibility of creating a home for himself according to his own taste through work and diligence, such a system does not regard him as a living co-creator in the great order directed toward the general welfare. For this system, he is a useful but completely unimportant object, a piece of material in the service of the general machinery of the State..

That was the first impression of our soldiers. They immediately got a correct picture. But it did not show all sides of Bolshevism. Here, therefore, follows a brief overview of its most important traits. In doing so, we always contrast our ideals with the Bolshevik machinations. We ask:

What is the difference between Bolshevism and National Socialism?

II. Against the old deception of the "equality" of all people we set the thesis of blood and race.

The false doctrine of the equality of all men is already very old. The United States Declaration of Independence (1776) begins, "All men are created equal." - The French Revolution of 1789 proclaimed "liberty, equality, and fraternity" as "human rights."

The fraud of human equality has brought disaster to the world for centuries: it led politically to "democracy ", economically to liberalism . Finally, Marxism also demands economic equality of all, that is, equalization of all incomes and wages. For this demand the workers of all countries should go into class struggle against the propertied classes. Bolshevism, likewise based on the deception of equality, wants to transform the whole of mankind into a unified world proletariat, which has to obey the Jewish-Bolshevik leadership without any will.

The false doctrine of equality violates the laws of nature. Everyone who opens his eyes realizes that people are not equal to each other. There are wise and limited, strong and weak, brave and fearful, etc. Even the peoples are not equal to each other. Those who have fought in Norway and Serbia, in France and Russia, can name numerous differences between the peoples. What are they?

It has also been scientifically proven for a long time that every human being is determined in his dispositions by the genetic makeup of his ancestors. The hereditary genes which prove this are important for our worldview. They bring down all the above-mentioned false doctrines. Just as individual human beings carry the hereditary material of their ancestors within themselves, so the predispositions of a people are explained by the roots from which it is formed. Even the peoples are not equal to each other.

The doctrine of the equality of peoples is a dangerous lie that has brought untold disaster upon the world.

III. Bolshevism Promotes Miscegenation - We Fight for the Purity of Blood

The world revolution striven for by Bolshevism is to be the melting pot in which everything that distinguishes the peoples from each other is to disappear: everything high and noble, family, clan, homeland, culture, religion. The blood-bound, soil- and homeland-rootedness of the Aryan man is the main obstacle for the Jewish plans of world domination. Therefore, among the peoples of the Soviet Union, race-mixing is favoured in every way. National Socialism demands purity of blood from the German people. If the blood is corrupted, the people die. History has taught us for ages the devastating consequences of racial mixing: Goths and Vandals in the Migration Period.

National Socialism therefore ensures the purity of the blood through education, but also through laws and regulations: "*Law for the Protection of German Blood and German Honour*". It provides protection against mixing with foreign blood, especially Jewish blood. - The German soldier abroad may marry only women of the Germanic people's; even these only with special permission.

".. .a racially pure people, which is conscious of its own blood will never be able to be subjugated by the Jew. The Jew will only be the master of bast will be in this world eternally only the master of bastards."
Adolf Hitler

IV. Against the Bolshevik oppression of high quality people, National Socialism sets personality and leadership.

For the realisation of its aims, Bolshevism needs a soulless mass of people, not creative personalities who could rebel against the Jewish-Bolshevik yoke. Therefore, it is important to him to extinguish (to "liquidate") the racially valuable forces of each people. Thus the leadership of tsarist Russia (scholars and officers, citizens and peasants) has been liquidated. This is how the high-quality people of the subjugated peoples are liquidated in large numbers (Katyn!). Bolshevism is simply afraid to let individuals grow out of the mass, Therefore, there is only one opinion in the Soviet Union: the opinion of Stalin. The overcrowded prisons and the years of misery in Siberia tell about the Bolshevik methods against those who somehow "stand out". In contrast, it is in the nature of National Socialism that it singles out the best minds. It rejects the doctrine of equality; that is why it has eliminated majority decisions everywhere (in people's representations, etc.). In the leadership of the state, in every office, in every enterprise, the most competent head is to be in charge.

The others form his followers. National Socialism therefore needs the most valuable personalities for leadership. It therefore consciously promotes them and places them in the decisive positions in all areas of life.

"The best form of society is the one which, with certainty, can bring the best minds of the national community to leading importance and guiding influence"

Adolf Hitler

V. Against Bolshevik egalitarianism and the exploitation of the working man, we place the socialism of Achievement

Bolshevism degrades the worker to the status of a working machine. The desired dictatorship of the proletariat is in reality a dictatorship of world Jewry, mixed with Asiatic despotism. The proceeds of labour, of course, do not benefit the working people. For more than twenty years all the proceeds have been taken from the people and put into the rebellion with which they now want to enforce the Jewish-Bolshevik world Jewry. This explains the misery that the German soldier perceives in the Soviet Union.

National Socialism, on the other hand, establishes the socialism of achievement. Since people are not equal, neither are benefits. Thus, economic equality contradicts the laws of life. National Socialism therefore does not demand equal pay for all, but rather equal opportunities for advancement. This is the solution to the long-contested social question. All the obstacles that have hitherto stood in the way of advancement for the dispossessed are torn down by National Socialism. Everyone has the same start for advancement. How far he gets depends on his abilities, his diligence, his willpower. - The esteem in which the individual is held in the national community is not determined by how far he climbs the economic ladder, but by how he uses the gifts given to him by nature. It is not what he does that is important, but how he does it. - Every worker is paid in such a way that he can participate in the cultural life of the people as an educated and equal fellow citizen. In economic life, too, there is a natural relationship between the employer and the employee based on performance. Both are at the service of the whole and are indispensable. This socialism of achievement guarantees not only a just selection but also the highest progress of economic life.

The Soviet Russian worker is a slave of the state; the National Socialist worker is a respected, equal member of the people.

VI. Against the soulless, mechanical concept of the state of Bolshevism, National Socialism sets the folkish state based on kinship.

Bolshevik man exists through and for the state. There is no goal in life except the state. Bolshevism does not know freedom and human dignity or religion. It destroys everything that makes life worth living for us. It wants no deeper ties and duties to fellow human beings, only those to the state. The family is considered a capitalist-bourgeois form of life and must be smashed.

National Socialism does not put the state first, but the people, and in the people the families. It fights for its people and thus for its kin; it works for its family and thus for its folk. But clan and family are rooted in the homeland. The National Socialist knows that life is bound by blood and soil. For the National Socialist, the state is only there for the sake of the people. The state is the organised people.

The Bolshevik state demands that freedom, homeland and family be sacrificed to it. The National Socialist fights for his own nation and is committed to freedom, homeland and family.

VII. Against the Judeo-Bolshevik world State National Socialism sets the organised Order of Europe with the Reich.

Bolshevism has consciously taken over the tradition of tsarist imperialism. Ever since Peter the Great, the masses from the East have been racing against Europe. For more than 300 years, the spectre of Russian mass attack has been growing on Europe's eastern frontier. Today, however, this threat has a double face. In its combination of Jewish Bolshevism and imperialist tradition, it is revolutionary and at the same time politically dangerous for Europe.

Like all imperialism, Soviet Russian imperialism wants to dominate, subjugate and exploit, just as one can subjugate and exploit slaves who have no honour; moreover, Bolshevik imperialism, by its methods of massification and racial mixing, wants to weaken the people. A people that loves its own honour and dignifies the honour of others seeks another form of coexistence among peoples.

Thus, we National Socialists are striving for the "Reich" as an organisation of cooperation between the European peoples, similar to the one we have already realised within our national community. Not only the Germanic sword and the fighting power of our divisions alone will determine the borders of this Reich, but the confidence of the other peoples in the mission of the Reich. To win this confidence and to be worthy of it is our immense political task.

Soviet imperialism wants to subjugate;

The "Reich" wants to lead.

Reference :

Adolf Hitler, "Mein Kampf," pp. 492-503;

"Europe and Bolshevism;

"Fighting Bolshevism

Lesson 15

Britain disturbs the peace of Europe

Why is Britain fighting against the Reich and a united Europe ?

In spite of the fact that this Germany was for decades the surest guarantor of peace and devoted herself only to her peaceful occupation, she has not been able to prevent other nations and especially their statesmen from pursuing this rise with envy and hatred and finally answering it with war."

Adolf Hitler , April 8, 1939

I. Britain has been the troublemaker of Europe for centuries

Since the beginning of the modern age, Britain has been engaged in overseas trade and has been brutally and ruthlessly attacking every other country with wars: Spain is defeated in alliance with Holland, Holland with France, France with Germany and Russia, Russia with France, Germany in the First World War with Russia, France, and so on.

II. For what reason and with what moral-religious justification is Britain waging these wars?

Two political reasons: to cover Britain's back in its unrestrained expansion into the world; trade monopoly, the sole prerogative to supply Europe with goods from overseas (arbitrary exploitation of Europe).

Moral Justification: Cromwell's Puritanism hammers into the British that they are called by God as a master nation to lead immature peoples. *"Britain is the instrument of God for the liberation and achievement of mankind."*

III. Where does Britain get the power to wage these wars?

It gains its power from the ideological-puritanical underpinnings of political soldiering; it finds support through the lie of "European balance"; Germany is its inexhaustible human reservoir for its mercenary armies.

IV. Why has Britain been fighting the Reich for 30 years?

First, in 1914, for the same reasons as before: it feels threatened by Germany in its rear and its world trade monopoly endangered. Secondly, World War Two in 1939, international antagonisms were a decisive factor.

V. Why did Britain foment the first world war in 1914?

Britain was unconcerned about the founding of the Second Reich (1864, 1866, 1870/71). At that time, foreign countries (India, Balkans, Near East) and especially France, which under Napoleon III strives for the old leadership position and builds up its second colonial empire, seem more important to him. Thus, the day of Sedan is not unwelcome for him.

Unexpectedly Germany's success came quickly. Bismarck at the Berlin Congress in 1878 as the "honest broker" organiser of European peace. Proposals for alliances in 1898 and 1901. Britain tries to drag the Reich into following its policy. Germany refuses to be drawn into a European war like Frederick the Great as a "continental daredevil" on Britain's behalf. But soon Britain's attitude changes; it sees its position as a world power threatened by the German Empire:

1. The strong German fleet appears as a threat to the nearby British coast.

2. The increase in trade, which is much steeper than that of Britain. Germany's share of the world .... trade is rising at the expense of Britain.

3. The newly established German colonial empire represents an interruption of the Cape-Cairo line of . ..dominance.

4. The economic advance of Germany in the direction of Berlin - Baghdad is directed into the flank of the British line Cairo - Calcutta and into the heart of the British Empire, India.

Edward VII completes the encirclement of Germany: 1904 Entente cordiale between Britain and France, 1907/09 Anglo-Russian understanding. The war, waged on the orders of and in the service of Jewry, is continued after the 1918 election with other means, in full recognition of the inherent powers of the German people. The brutal pressure triggers - highly undesirable for Britain - the National Socialist revolution of 1933.

VI. What drives Britain to declare war in 1939?

By the surrender of its former allies, Poland, etc., to the Soviet Union, Britain is exposed. No longer does anyone believe that Britain went into battle for the freedom of small peoples and for democracy. Britain has recognized that a new world is in the making, the world of the unbridled manic soul which is wrestling itself free from the Jewish world of the British-American world economic system. What are now - apart from the always unchanging economic worries - the unchanged ideological differences between the two worlds?

1. The hysterical attitude of the British ruling class, oversaturated in possessions, which is losing its fighting spirit, before the elemental outbreak of the Nordic spirit in young Germany.

2. The racial and ethnic question.

Germany, through her race policy, has taken up the fight against the greatest danger to all European peoples, racial death by mixing with races foreign to her species. No people of Europe, indeed of the whole world, can fail to take a stand on this question. In Britain, too, this realisation seems to be dawning. The British ruling class is resisting this, for it is so closely bound to Judaism by blood and especially by ideology that a separation without the unification of the plutocratic system is unthinkable.

3 German Socialism:

The right to work and life for every member of the German national community is a threat to the dominant economic conception in Britain: according to the Jewish-Puritan-liberalist conception, every individual has to fight the battle of life for himself. The haves are blessed by God, the poor rejected. Plutocracy and misery, which in our view make a mockery of all social justice, are, in the British view, willed by God. *"Common good comes before self-interest"* is incomprehensible to the British businessman.

4 The elimination of the division of peoples into "haves" and "have-nots," the demand of Germany for colonies and for the just distribution of raw materials in the colonial countries, for free participation in world trade, seems to the British a presumption; for in their view God's blessing decides on the wealth of the nations. The have-nots are obviously rejected by God.

5 The Realisation of the All-German Idea

Through the creation of the Greater German Reich, the chains of Versailles have been broken; in place of the political void in Central Europe has emerged a powerful people's state, renouncing British tutelage.

6 The Reich discovers its two-thousand-year mission as a regulatory power in Europe. It hereby opposes the British arrogance of being called by God to world domination. Europe is to cease to be an object of British exploitation and to tear each other apart at British orders.

Europe for the Europeans, not for the British.

Conclusion:

Throughout the centuries in which it has exercised a decisive influence on European politics, Britain has proved that it has no interest in Europe. It has constantly stirred up the peoples against each other with the lie of European balance of power and then left them in the mud. It sees in Europe only a project of exploitation. It is the element of destruction, not of order and construction.

The greatest danger for the British today is a unified Europe under German leadership. It will then no longer be in a position to exploit the continent. It will drop out of the European family of nations, or it will be given the right to be a nation among nations.

SS HANDBLÄTTER
FÜR DEN WELTANSCHAULICHEN UNTERRICHT

Lesson 16

British imperialism in the struggle against the Reich as the European power of order

How does the German claim to leadership differ from the British idea of world domination?

"And the German people will not be splintered somehow by this struggle, but it will become firmer and firmer. If anything splinters, it will be the states, which themselves are so un-homogeneously (non-uniformly) composed as our plutocratic world democracies, these so-called world empires, which themselves are built only on oppression of peoples and domination of peoples."

Adolf Hitler

I. Two views

These views are opposed to each other. They are indicative of the grounds of the struggle in which we stand today.

The Briton says: I am a member of the chosen people who, for their benefit, must conquer the world from the hands of barbarian peoples for the sake of world commerce, for the sake of Christianity, and for the sake of their culture as God wills.

The German says: For my people I fight to preserve its life and its holy soil, highest values of culture, to preserve its deep reverent faith in justice, in freedom and personality for all times and hereby to save Europe from ruin.

II. Two adversaries

The German Reich and the British Empire, abysmally different in attitude and outlook. A struggle of world-historical decision between two worlds.

III. The German Imperial Idea is as Old as the Germanic-German World

Armin, first attempt of a summary in Northern Germany. Theoderich attempts a union of all Germanic peoples, the first prince of peace and order for Europe.

Charlemagne: unites for the first time all the present-day German tribes, forcibly, but the idea remains.

Henry I. 919, founder of the first Reich. Peaceful, without the intervention of the church. The Reich is 1. national unity, 2. European power of order.

The great Kaisers of the Middle Ages, 10th-13th centuries, bequeathed the idea of empire to the German people as a political testament, as a belief and as a goal. This idea is the dream of the Germans and the hope of Europe, the strongest formative force of the continent.

IV. On what is the German sense of mission based?

a) On the historical achievement of the German people; culturally, it creates the European culture of the Middle Ages out of the decaying world of antiquity from the Germanic spirit.

The world of states after the migration of peoples is founded throughout by Germanic peoples.

The protection of Europe against foreign invasions, culturally and militarily, ultimately rests, after overrunning the external positions, always with the German people (e.g. against Huns, Avars, Hungarians, Tatars, Mongols, Turks, etc.).

b) Today the Reich bears the main burden of the struggle.

Weltanschaulich (Worldview): all other peoples of Europe have more or less fallen into the Jewish-liberalistic spirit. In contrast, the Reich holds fast to the Nordic ideals: honour and loyalty, achievement, leadership, species-conscious peasantry, socialism of action.

(Geo) Politically: Because of its central position it comes into contact with all peoples of Europe and thus participates in the European destinies in North and South, in East and West. It mediates economically and culturally between the other peoples and has the greatest capacity to absorb all European problems.

In terms of racial and numerical strength, it is the greatest powerhouse in Europe.

V. British Imperialism

Is based on the divine mission consciousness of Puritanism. Britain is the people chosen by God to make the world happy..

Comparison with Judaism.

British imperialism builds its empire by violent means. Examples:

Ireland, enslaved for centuries, the only European nation whose population declined in the 19th century.

The Indians: Brutal subjugation for the purpose of exploiting the richest country in the world. For centuries, pitiless against the famines.

China: Forced introduction of opium poison in the Opium War.

The Boers: The brave Boer people are subjugated only out of capitalist greed for profit. When the weapons fail: last means of violence the concentration camps.

First and second world wars: Starvation blockade, terror bombing.

VI. summary

The Reich was always aware of its European task.

The Reich has defended Europe against the Orient, against the Huns and Mongols, against storms from the southeast as well as from Africa. And the Reich has defended the freedom of the Nordic-Germanic spirit against the spiritual imperialism of the Papacy.

Britain's policy was never a service to the European continent, but a constant struggle against a united Europe. National-bound German socialism was and is a danger to the British idea of world domination. This war is the tremendous confrontation of worldviews which are implacably and irreconcilably opposed to each other.

Britain wants to rule! The Reich wants to lead!

Reference :

"The Reich and Europe"

Lesson 17

U.S.A. stooge of the Jewish world power

> *"The forces carrying Mr. Roosevelt were the forces which I fought on the basis of the destiny of my people and my most sacred inner conviction. The 'brain trust' of which the new American President had to avail himself was composed of members of the same people whom we fought as a parasitic phenomenon of humanity in Germany and began to remove from public Lesson life."*

> The Führer in his Reichstag speech on 11.12.1941

How is it that today the Jew largely determines the fate of America, which is predominantly populated by Europeans ?

I. Settlement of USA

America was first discovered by Norwegian navigators around the year 1000. At the end of the 15th century, Europeans again set foot on American soil (Columbus).In 1507, the German cartographer Waldseemüller coined for this new country the name America after Amerigo Vespucci, a companion of Columbus.

In the course of the 17th century began that tremendous process of colonisation, which in the following centuries filled this continent mainly with people from Europe. Among the first immigrants were especially many people who were looking for a new home because of their faith or their political convictions. These immigrants, mainly from Britain and France, brought with them the Puritan-Calvinist spirit that became the general outlook on life.

II. Puritanism and Judaism

The Puritans based their views especially on the Old Testament and adopted many habits of life from the requirements it contained for the Jewish people. They did not realise that in so doing they were adopting content which must have been contrary to their racial feelings.

The Puritans were also the origin of that fatal trait of the entire Anglo-American world which wants to see the relations between God and man regulated by contract. It is that spirit which, in its exaggeration, has today become the justification for all the actions of every American. *"God gave me my money,"* says Rockefeller. According to the Puritans, one is either chosen by God or rejected. Divine grace is especially revealed in the business successes one achieves.

When such thinking is commonplace among a population, there is no understanding of social problems. Poverty, unemployment, not getting ahead in business are manifestations of divine disgrace. Therefore, until a few years ago, there was no state welfare, no unemployment insurance of any kind.

These examples show the fatal relationship between the Puritan and the Jewish conception of the task of life. Here as there, the mission of God Yahweh to his "Chosen People" to rule over the whole world is taken seriously. Here as there, the relationship to this God has been shaped into a relationship of purpose. Both are happy with any means to achieve their goals, which they use in the most unscrupulous way, always carried by the pleasant feeling that they are also doing the bad and vile things on behalf of their god, as whose instrument they feel themselves to be.

III. Increased Penetration of the Jews

Towards the end of the 19th century, immigrants also came more and more from other parts of the world. The consequent interspersion of the American population with foreign races was especially marked by the rapidly increasing immigration of Jews and by the rapidly increasing numbers of the Negro population.

The racial melting pot was intended to create "American people."

By the turn of the century, the problems associated with this were already becoming so apparent that people were frantically searching for a way out of this mess. The solution seemed to have been found in a little play by the Jew Israel Zangwill, which was performed in 1909. It was called "The Crucible". It was now believed that this "melting pot" could overcome the lack of racial uniformity and a slowly and healthily grown tradition, the lack of consciousness of a unified folk, and that this "melting pot America" was capable of erasing all racial differences and bringing about the emergence of the "American man."

Racial chaos is a prerequisite for the leadership role of the Jews.

By this view the victory of a secret longing of the Jews had become manifest. For they, who could not assert themselves as a unified tribe in any state of the world, and whose goal is the subjugation of the whole world under their rule, could now direct this mishmash of people wanted by the government and public opinion according to their will, and thus gain control of the world.

And thus secure for themselves the leadership of this continent.

U.S. Heavy industry about				87%,
U.S. Banking about ...	.	.	.	100%
U.S. Export trade .	.	.	.	90 %

U.S. Newspapers .	.	.	.	97 %
U.S.Textile industry .	.	.	.	99 %
U.S. Land .	.	.	.	62 %

in Jewish hands or at least under Jewish control.   Thus the Jews have the predominance in those economic fields from which, by appropriate control, the formation of public opinion can be largely influenced by appropriate control

In addition to their strong influence in the field of foreign policy and the formation of political opinion in general, the Jews are absolutely leading in the field of theatre and film. Thus the Jews possess further excellent means of influencing public opinion. Even before the entry of the U.S.A. into the present great ideological war, more than 24 anti-German inflammatory films were made by the Jewish film companies!

IV. Americanism – the destruction of all culture

The Jewish-Puritan striving for power, property and wealth, together with the ever-increasing racial chaos, had the consequence that the need for cultural things, from which a racially unified and bloodily healthy people draws an essential part of its life and creative energy, became less and less. Adolf Hitler said on May 1, 1933: ***"What there is of real values of human culture did not arise from internationalism, but the Volkstum created it."*** In the failure of these preconditions lies for us also the key to the realisation of the flattening of American culture and its decisive turn to unculture. Controlled by the Jews, the multitude of peoples and races in the U.S.A. grew into only pseudo-values and a pseudo-worldview of "Americanism", the basis of which is the consciousness of being chosen.

The inner emptiness of the American express's itself in the standardisation of all life processes, in the meaningless phrase, the sweet but empty smile, in the jazz melody, in the pop song and in the "tin can". In nothing must the problems of life be touched!

Summary of American cultural life:

Genuine feeling has been replaced by sentimentality, the high ethics of European culture by soulless mass performances. How right our Führer is when he makes the demand for Germany: ***"We must educate a new man, so that our people will not perish from the typical degenerative aspects of this new age."***

V. Jewish-Puritan economic form

The American economy is built on this cultural standard of living and on the political-ideological theses. Its basic trait is the Puritan acquisitiveness. Cheap labour without social justice, unrestrained exploitation of the soil and its treasures. In addition to the lack of ability, there is also the lack of will on the part of the puritanical Jewish ruling class to put the social problems in order. The German worker knows that he is fighting as a free citizen and as a comrade of the people for a genuine socialism; the American worker is forced to work for the world domination plans of the Jewish plutocracy.

VI. Roosevelt's Plans for World Domination

It was out of this Jewish Puritan spirit that Roosevelt proclaimed his ambition of world domination. His stealthy, cautious, and deceptive step-by-step policy led America into this great war.

In 1933, Roosevelt affirmed his administration's firm resolve to remain neutral. In the following years, a moral partisanship against National Socialism began, which strongly endangered the international, Jewish-capitalist oriented economic form of America.

In 1939, the U.S. public was prepared for the possibility of a conflict. On October 31, 1940, shortly before his re-election, this did not prevent the President from declaring that America would not participate in foreign wars.

After re-election, he could now pursue more openly his policy of threats against the Reich, which eventually led to war against the Reich and Europe.

Thus, a large white continent serves the Jew to complete their plans for world domination!

VII. Our task

The values which America has written on its banner in the name of democracy and for the protection of the freedom of peoples are clever camouflages of the Jewish-American intentions of world domination. Therefore, we oppose Americanism with the following basic attitude:

> Folk and family of folk against racial chaos!
>
> Blood-bound socialism against capitalism!
>
> Personality against massification!
>
> Culture against entertainment technology!
>
> Commitment to the soil against robbery of the soil!
>
> Peasantry against capitalist farming!
>
> Nordic attitude of destiny against happy-end!

Under the leadership of the Reich, the peoples of Europe are not only defending their ancient culture, but are also fighting for a worldview which, must and will, overcome the Jewish-American plans for world domination!

"We know what force is behind Roosevelt. It is that eternal Jew who considers his time has come to carry out also on us what we all had to see and experience shuddering in Soviet Russia. We have now become acquainted with the Jewish paradise on earth. Millions of German soldiers have been able to gain a personal impression of a country in which this international Jew destroyed and annihilated people and property."

Der Führer on December 11, 1941

Reference :

1. "The Dollar Rolls."

2. "Americanism - A World Danger."

SS HANDBLÄTTER
FÜR DEN WELTANSCHAULICHEN UNTERRICHT

Lesson 18

The Jew destroys every national order of life

"If the international financial Jewry inside and outside Europe should succeed in plunging the peoples once more into a world war, the result will not be the Bolshevization of the earth and thus the victory of Jewry, but the annihilation of the Jewish race in Europe."

The Führer on January 30, 1939.

Jewry has shown in the course of its four thousand years of history that it is neither able nor willing to build and maintain an orderly state of its own. It is scattered all over the world and lives, like germs, only from other peoples, until it has absorbed them and brought them to the abyss. On the ruins of these peoples the Jew wants to build world domination. The present war in particular is a struggle of decomposing Jewry against healthy, vital peoples who, on the basis of their race, blood and nature, have the strength to build up their own, precisely a folkish order.

I. Judaism strives for world domination. This lies in its worldview

The political goal of the Jew is an international world state, the domination of all peoples, no matter to what race they belong, what their ethnic characteristics may be. This striving for world domination lies in his religious idea to be the "chosen people of God". For example, it speaks from the 5th book of Moses:

"But all the nations which Yahweh thy God giveth thee shall thou destroy, without looking pityingly on them; and their gods thou shalt not worship: for that would be a snare unto thee."

The Jew, according to his religious laws, regards every stranger as an Other, as an inhuman being whom he can exploit, exploit and then dominate to his advantage.

II. The two main poisons with which Judaism creeps into the ideas of the peoples are materialism and individualism

1. What is materialism?

Materialism is a worldview which recognises only material things as real and regards all mental and spiritual processes as material. The enjoyment of the external goods of life is the meaning and purpose of life. Thus materialism has no sense for values of character, for the moral personality. Human life is meaningless and indifferent, and thus the national community is also meaningless. Materialism denies the existence of basic racial ethnic forces.

2 What is individualism?

Individualism holds that only the individual has meaning and value. The original essence of human society is the individual detached from the community. The emphasis on the ego results in an overestimation of the dissecting intellect, a one-sided view of all life that is not subject to any purpose. The unbridled greed for profit of the irresponsible and rootless individual ego.

III. The Jew contaminates and breaks up the order of life of his host peoples. The prime example is Germany before the assumption of power.

How the Jew has always made the leading peoples of the world, except Japan, largely compliant, will be shown by the points which are the most important expressions of life of all cultural peoples: the economy, the state, the culture, the customs and the law. The prime example, unfortunately, is Germany until the assumption of power.

1. The Jew, through the control of money, commerce, banking, and business, consolidates his mastery of the world economy

Through the Jew prevails the idea that money is in and of itself a power. The Jewish religion already praises wealth as the highest good; for the Jew, money is the goal of his life. The god of the Jews is money.

How does the Jew dominate the economy in banking and the stock exchange?

Jewish high finance serves in the whole world only the Jewish interest to the detriment and exploitation of all nations. He wants to get control of production and consumption of the whole world in his hand, so that every nation is dependent on him.

2. The Jew, with the help of Freemasonry, revolutions, democracy and parliamentarism, is ransacking the national organisation of every community, every state.

Scattered for 2,000 years and condemned to their own tribe's powerlessness, the Jews have always been dogged carriers of indignation. That is why they have run all modern revolutions (in South America, Portugal, Hungary, Russia, Spain). The Jews were active in all secret societies, especially in

Freemasonry, which then drove to the French Revolution in 1789. Spreading of the fatal doctrine of "equality of all that is human". Equality of all peoples and races. From 1848 on, the Jewish influence becomes more and more palpable in all revolutions. The revolutionary storm at the end of the World War over Europe was ignited by Jews, also that of the German Revolution of 1918. - After the fall of the imperial government, the Jews suddenly forced their way into the governmental offices.

3. The Jew degenerates all national culture and uses it for propaganda for his own international plans.

In countless books, Jewish writers have mocked the highest and holiest goods of the nation, have glorified sedition, treason against the Fatherland, moral licentiousness and egoism.

These Jewish writers could never have attained their devastating influence if they had not been generously promoted by the Jewish press. The Jew also uses the press for his stock exchange business. He alerts the people to impending crises, bad harvests, wars, etc.. In this way he achieves that his agricultural products are bought in considerably larger quantities. The Jew then rapidly increases the prices, and so he does his business to the detriment of the hard-working and honest people.

Theatre, film and the performing arts in Germany were also widely dominated by the Jewish minority. Often this "art" was nothing more than Bolshevik propaganda, a mockery of national dignity and honour, blasphemy of military discipline and the idea of defence. The Jew dictated his culture to us!

4. The Jew undermines sociality and thus weakens the discipline, culture and child wealth of the nation.

The Jewish addiction to sensual and effeminate enjoyment of life. Systematic immorality of youth through inappropriate teaching, through exaggerated unnatural sensuality in speech, writing and pictures. Organised destruction of family life. One-child system. Reduction of the number of children. Protection of one's own wife, racial desecration of Aryan women. In contrast to this is the folkish state, as the National Socialist state is to a marked degree, with its deliberate promotion of the number of births.

"At the top of the assessment of success stands the German child, stands our youth, stands the birth rate. If that grows, then I know that our people will not perish and our work will not have been in vain."

The Führer

5. The Jewish criminal nature perverts and displaces every law and justice.

We Germans stand on the folkish point of view: right is what benefits the people, wrong is what harms the people.

With a calculating mind, the Jew constructs a "rational" legal system that is supposed to be suitable for all peoples and for all times.

The only valid legal book of the Jews gives Judaism carte blanche for every disgraceful deed and for every crime up to the coldly calculated cowardly murder of non-Jews, if the deed benefits the Jew. One thinks here of the murder of the National Socialist Gauleiter Wilhelm Gustloff in Davos by the Jew David Frankfurter (1936) and of the murder of the German diplomat Ernst vom Rath in Paris by the Jew Herschel Grynzspan (1938).

IV. The Jew is the Instigator and Prolonger of the Present War

1 The Russian Bolshevism is a manifestation of Jewish thought.

What does Bolshevism look like in Russia?

Russia was an agrarian state, and compared to agriculture, industry did not play a significant role. Hence the fight of the Jew, who by blood is an opponent of all land owning , for the destruction of the peasantry.

Stalin abolished the small-scale peasant economy, and the large-scale collective was to take its place. The peasant must be reduced to a farm labourer. Through electoral reform, the peasantry was deprived of all political influence. The peasant was branded as the class enemy of the worker, and the workers for their part were turned into proletarians. The ultimate aim was to turn the countries of Europe into labour provinces for international Jewry. The preliminary aim, however, was a giant industry for the purpose of arming for a world war and thus for carrying out a world revolution!

The peasants, who allowed themselves to be forced into the collective, thus went into slavery. This is how the famine came about in 1929. In order to control this deplorable state of affairs and to increase the number of state farms, Stalin resorted to the sharpest means: mass murder. The harvest was secured with the help of the Red Army then the Jew exported at usurious prices and did business with the products that the peasant had produced under forced labour, even though the peasants of the country were starving.

For the grain had to bring in foreign exchange, and the foreign exchange was necessary for the procurement of machines for the armaments industry, i.e., for the procurement of weapons for the world revolution.

Now what is the worldview of Bolshevism?

Bolshevism is an outgrowth of genuine Jewish thinking! See the men around Lenin and Stalin.

If Marxism, with its doctrine of class struggle, was to pave the way to power for Jewry on European soil, the Jew devised Bolshevism as the instrument with which he could force victory over the peoples of the Russian area. From there he wanted to fight down and dominate Europe.

Bolshevism is a radical modernist view of the world. It first tore the concept of God out of the hearts of the Russian people, which had actually been the only content of their uncomplicated soul life. In doing so, he took away every value of the human being and every higher meaning of life. He reduced man to a production machine.

The disenchantment of the masses of millions in Russia. Bolshevism also wants to rob the peoples of Europe of their culture and turn them into a general human mass. It exterminates the racially valuable people of each nation.

2. The Jew supports the British Imperialism

The unity of the continent, which our arms seek to fight for, is threatened in the West by the British island. The threat is actually not the British people, but British imperialism: the will to rule and oppress of a relatively small stratum. This stratum is as much Jewish as British! In Britain, Jewry supports the rule of the upper classes, enters into it and leads the struggle for its interests: its wealth and its power in Europe. The British leaders are thus mixed with the groups of the Jewish people in whom the thought of Jewish world rule lives and works.

3. The Jew is behind American plutocracy

Just as in Britain, however, Jewry also wants to realise its plans of domination through the final success in this war under the mask of democratic, free America as well as under the larva of Bolshevik world happiness.

The folk recognise their common enemy and are ready to fight against the Jew.

V. Conclusion

If Bolshevism were to succeed in breaking through the living wall of our bodies on the Eastern Front and in flooding Europe, the end of the culture of the European peoples would be at hand.

For Germany there is only one goal: fight Bolshevism and fight the plutocracies. Eradicate the Jew, the arch-enemy of every nation! And for the new Europe, which will arise under the leadership of Germany on the basis of a peoples' order after the final victory, there can only be one slogan:

"Liberation of Europe from the rule of the Jew!"

SS HANDBLÄTTER

FÜR DEN WELTANSCHAULICHEN UNTERRICHT

Lesson 19

The Freemasons, Instrument of World Jewry

Freemasonry is the secret order of world Judaism for the attainment of world domination

> *"In order to strengthen his political position, the Jew tries to tear down the racial and civic barriers which at first still restrict him at every turn. To this end, he fights with all his characteristic tenacity for religious tolerance and has in Freemasonry, which is completely in thrall to him, a ready instrument for championing his aims as well as for pushing them through. The circles of the ruling classes as well as the higher strata of the political and economic bourgeoisie get into its snares through masonic threads, without their even having to suspect it."*

Adolf Hitler

I. Historical development of Freemasonry

In the Middle Ages, the guilds of stonemasons and masons were held in high esteem by kings, princes and the people. The guilds of builders, travelled from country to country as closed groups under the leadership of their master builder (cathedral builder) and built the enormous works of the Middle Ages which we still admire today (Cathedrals, Imperial palaces, Town halls, Arsenals, Storehouses etc.) on behalf of Emperors, Kings, Princes, Bishops or Cities.

The members of the building lodges had certain distinctive signs that reminded them of their common activity and their togetherness (square, compass, trowel, hammer, apron), as well as secret forms of greeting.

These building lodges unintentionally became the starting point for today's freemasonry. The building lodges came into contact with medieval secret societies of a political, religious and other nature. Through the emerging custom of admitting non-masons to the guilds, political obscurantists and secret alliance forces penetrated, alienated the guilds and turned them into a cover for secret subversive ideas.

When the building lodges fell into disrepair as a result of the 30 Years' War, in 1717 the British added four building lodges that still existed in London under the name of "Lodge" (Lodge). The first Grand Lodge was thus created, and from this time onwards a tight organisation of international Freemasonry can be traced.

The Masonic Lodge was founded in Britain in 1717 and developed from the building lodges of the Middle Ages, after the good spirit of work masonry had been changed into the dark political aims of spiritual masonry.

II. The Nature of Freemasonry

Freemasonry fights for freedom, equality, fraternity of all men, i.e., for general brotherhood of man. Like Bolshevism, Freemasonry liberates people from the natural bonds of race, people and nation and makes them citizens of the world.

After 1717, Freemasonry spread to all countries of the world; lodges sprang up everywhere. Men in influential positions were preferentially drawn into the lodges. Once one had taken the oath, one was forever a slave to Freemasonry. Resignation did not release one from the oath and the duty of secrecy and did not protect one from revenge.

All the lodges of the world are international. Freemasonry has been as unwilling to admit this as it has been to admit its political aims. Deceptively, it often wrote nationalism on its banners. All camouflage and lies. The Freemason Horneffer writes: *"Whoever joins a lawfully constituted Lodge, in whatever place, becomes a member of the whole Confederation of World Freemasonry."* In principle, all Lodges in the world are somehow incorporated into the organisation of official World Freemasonry, and thus all Lodges are international. "National Lodges" are therefore lies.

Freemasonry claims to promote religiosity. Also a lie. The truth is that it is an enemy of all confessions and that it recognises in "humanity" the equalising religion of all peoples.

The claim that many lodges are Christian is also a cover. Proof: Wherever Freemasons gained political leadership, they proceeded with violence against Christianity. Thus in the French Revolution of 1789, where reason was elevated to the status of goddess, thus in the last century in Italy the Grand Masters Garibaldi and Mazzini, thus the Freemasons Lenin, Trotsky and Stalin in Russia, likewise the Masonic governments in Mexico, Spain, Hungary (Béla Kun) and Greece (Venizelos). See also the Book of Constitutions of 1723: *"All Freemasons shall profess the religion in which all men agree, i.e., Freemasonry professes the idea of the equality of all that is human, consciously eliminating all that separates, such as race, religion and class"*

Freemasonry presents itself as a benefactor of humanity. It is true that she cared for the poor and dressed confirmation and communicant children every year. Reason: camouflage. What does it mean compared to our WHW and NSV?

Freemasonry talks about human ennoblement. We refrain from the ennoblement that makes people the criminal tools of international Jewish Freemasonry by oath. It talks of world peace or peace among nations. Impudent lie, for Freemasonry stirs up revolutions and wars.

It seeks to cultivate the life of society. But why does it do it? To put people under the influence of secret mysticism of pacifist and international ideas.

It denies that it is politically active, but the truth is that it interferes in all political events. Its ultimate goal is the political leadership of all peoples, i.e., world domination.

Summary: Freemasonry is an international secret society that seeks to dominate the world under the guise of the brotherhood of man.

III. Freemasonry - an instrument of Judaism

If international Freemasonry fought for the brotherhood of man, it could not exclude the Jew. The Jew would not have been a Jew if the doors to civil and state life had not been opened to him through membership of the Lodge. The emancipation of the Jews was the work of the Freemasons.

Soon Jewish influence in the lodges increased until it dominated them. The customs of the lodges became Jewish-oriented. The Freemason is educated in the Jewish spirit. It is essential that the lodges, which are in contact with each other, are subordinated in their entirety to a central Jewish leadership.

The more important and significant a Freemason is, the higher his rank (degree). In the higher degrees, world politics is pursued, and here crimes, wars and revolutions, murders of opponents, princes and politicians who have become disliked are instigated. The highest degree is the 33rd degree. The Supreme Council (one in each country) is formed from Brothers of the 33rd Degree. The Supreme Council is the most decisive political power factor in world Freemasonry, which conducts world politics of the greatest magnitude (Roosevelt, Rathenau).

Although most of the lodge brothers in the world are not Jews, this world-wide federation is nevertheless the most cunning organisation of Judaism; for Jews occupy up to 60 to 70 per cent of the high degrees.

The means for the achievement of the Jewish World Republic are, in the main, revolution, war and destruction through the capture of power, politics, government, and influence in all spheres of life. All revolutions since the founding of the lodges have been the work of Freemasons, with the exception of the National Socialist and Fascist revolutions.

Examples of lodge work: French Revolution of 1789.

1740-1790, 700 lodges were founded in France to prepare for the revolution. The intellectual pioneers such as Montesquieu, Diderot, Voltaire, Mirabeau, Danton, Robespierre were all Freemasons. The Lodge demanded the head of the King. Nordic elements were exterminated.

The encirclement of Germany before 1914 was the work of Freemasons. Freemasons orchestrated the murder in Sarajevo (instigating the First World War). The Dictate of Shame at Versailles was the result of a Lodge decision of 30 June 1917, passed in Paris. Our collapse in 1918 is also the work of the Freemasons. Ebert, Scheidemann, Kurt Eisner, Liebknecht, Rathenau and others were the Masonic guarantors of Jewry.

Marx, Trotsky, Lenin, the champions of Bolshevism, were also Freemasons, as were almost all the heads of state of the enemy powers: George VI, Churchill, Eden, Roosevelt (33rd degree), etc. Of the 18 members of the Grand Council who voted against the Duce's policy, 13 were Freemasons. King Emanuel and Badoglio are also Freemasons.

Thus Judah rules through world Freemasonry.

CONCLUSION : Through world Freemasonry, which belongs to Judaism, world Judaism seeks to establish the Jewish world state.

IV. Why National Socialism must fight against World Freemasonry

World Freemasonry	National Socialism
Negates people and race.	Makes people and race eternal values
Destroys the values of the species, educates to humanity	Cultivates the inherent values of the species educates for national community
Only a select clique, demands democracy as a form of government.	Embraces the people without distinction of class or education
Preaches peace among nations, but oppresses the peoples	Demands the state as a living structure of kindred people, cultivates military power power as guarantor of peace.
Speaks of charity, which is cultivated to a limited extent and in pretence	Created the National Socialist People's Welfare group, the Winter Help Campaign and the Mother and Child Programme etc.
Wants a world republic,	Belief in the Nation

World Freemasonry and National Socialism oppose each other like fire and water. Freemasonry sees its mortal enemies in National Socialism and in the racial awakening of the peoples. In Germany it is banned, but not dead. The strictest vigilance is necessary, especially in wartime. Masonic whispers (peace, pacifism, understanding, etc.) are supposed to put us to sleep; but they mean our downfall.

National Socialist measures against the Freemasons:

1. On 17 August 1935, the government ordered the dissolution of the last Freemason lodges in Germany (many had voluntarily disbanded by then).

2. Former members of Masonic lodges and lodge-like organisations may only be members of the NSDAP and its branches if they had resigned before 30 January 1933 and expressly affirm that they no longer feel bound by their vows to the lodges.

Conclusion :

National Socialism fights Freemasonry because through it Judaism wants to exterminate and enslave our nation.

SS
HANDBLÄTTER
FÜR DEN WELTANSCHAULICHEN UNTERRICHT

Lesson 20

This War is an Ideological War
The necessity for a political soldier

"This war is being waged so bitterly and mercilessly because it represents the decisive struggle between two worldviews".

Adolf Hitler [1]

Why is this war a battle of worldviews and what are the consequences for the German soldier?

I. The Clash of Worldviews

The present war is a battle of ideologies.

History teaches us that all great wars have not only been struggles for power, but rather wars of ideology. The history of the Reich is filled with the struggle for Germanic freedom and for the realisation of the national state (Peasants' Wars, Thirty Years' War [2]).

With the progressive mobilisation of the masses in the modern wars and the effectiveness of the supranational powers of Judaism and Freemasonry, the force of the great ideological struggle of the Reich experiences an unheard-of increase.

a) The German people, under the leadership of Adolf Hitler, have stood up to the world power of Judaism and the Freemasons. In what is the effectiveness of the Jewish spirit evident? What were the symptoms of illness from which all European peoples suffered and in some cases still suffer today?

The defeat of 1918 was also followed by an inner collapse of the German people. The germs of disease that had already been in our people before the beginning of the World War broke out into an open state of illness.

Even before the beginning of the World War, a view of life had taken hold in the people which valued the individual only in terms of money. This materialistic view of life seized our people after 1918 like a frenzy. Reckless acquisition of money appeared to be the highest ideal of life. Insane speculation on the stock exchange, carried out by banks and individuals, led to the impoverishment of the thrifty middle classes. In the midst of national misery and the degradation of our honour, an addiction to pleasure was spreading in the big cities that knew no bounds; delinquency among young people was increasing year by year, suicides were mounting as a result of the loss of faith in life.

A dissolution of the moral values, of faith, honour, reverence and loyalty, which had always been the basis of Germanic state life, went hand in hand with this disintegration of life. The children stood up against their parents, the pupils against their teachers, the youth against old age. Reverence for the great past of the German people was deliberately destroyed in the newspapers and in books written by Jews or people belonging to Jews. The heroic was dragged into the dust, the victims of the world war were ridiculed, the laws of blood were despised (increasing intermarriage of Aryan people with Jews and Jewish descendants). In art (theatre and music), the common and lowly aspects of human nature were highlighted and celebrated, and all sense of sacrifice and commitment to a greater cause were branded as ridiculous and outdated.

What followed was the destruction of the very foundations of the folkish society. The workers were incited against the employers, and the employers, oblivious to their duties, took advantage of the hardship and unemployment of their workers in order to pursue only their profits. Class hatred was preached. The state, which is supposed to be a mother for all, became a plaything in the hands of the parties and interest groups.

The depth of the ideological upheaval in Germany can only be grasped by those who have had a look into the abyss, facing our nation after 1918: the whole nation was threatened with racial death as a result of the restriction of the number of children, the destruction of the German culture, personal -honour and dissolution

Adolf Hitler's movement attacked the root of the evil by declaring war on Judaism and Freemasonry. Since Judaism and Freemasonry were about to seize power in all European countries, this declaration of war, which at first only served the recovery of their own fatherland, called world Jewry and world Freemasonry onto the scene, who felt threatened by this declaration of war .[3]

b) The supranational powers of Judaism and Freemasonry, which are working in all countries of Europe and America towards the destruction of national values, see themselves threatened by the emergence of National Socialism in Germany, and they are declaring war on the world in the hope that they will be able to reverse this trend.

Only in this way can the declarations of war by the great money powers and their alliances with Bolshevism, which also serves the realisation of the Jewish plan of world domination, be understood.

Britain has declared war on the Reich because the British plutocracy hates the German system of socialism, which gives everyone work and bread. The plutocratic liberalism of Britain is fighting its last battle in this war.

America has declared war on the Reich because it too fears the spread of socialist ideas on its continent from the state of Adolf Hitler, because it cannot itself offer a solution to the workers' question of the threat of unemployment after the war, and because European socialism is regarded by it as a threat to and limitation of the power of international capital. [4]

Jewry and Freemasonry in both countries have declared war on Europe because socialism emanating from the Reich is the strongest force of resistance against the intended exploitation of the European continent as a colony of the golden International. Judaism and Freemasonry, however, fall with the power of capital over the peoples and the individual.

Bolshevism has been preparing the war against Europe for 20 years, because it represents only the Asiatic form of international Jewish Marxism and believes that it can only maintain its own system of reducing man to a production machine by creating equal conditions in all countries of the world.

Bolshevism and Americanism, however, are the mortal enemies of the culture of our continent, of the order of all folk life on the basis of blood and race. Both worldviews agree that they result in the bastardisation of peoples, the massification of people and the degradation of man to a machine. [5]

In the present struggle, therefore, the great opposites of our modern life are clashing in alternating forms: culture against society, man against machine. The nobility of labour against enslavement, the people against. the international, the faith in God against. the devilish diabolism.   The acrimony and ruthlessness that accompanies this struggle in the military field is corresponding. The consequence of this is the unquestioned commitment of the German and European fighter to his worldview.

II. Conclusions from this historical insight

The struggle in which we are engaged requires of each individual not only the soldierly virtues of loyalty, obedience and bravery, but also, with imperative necessity, the politically fanatical soldier who recognises the ideological depth and breadth of the struggle in which we stand, and who is a good fighter for Germanic and European values.

1. The Bolshevik army is politically trained down to the smallest unit and in training as well as in warfare of movement and position.[6] *"The battle with the Russian enemy has justified our conviction that only those troops will be victorious in this war in the long run whose men are not only capable soldiers, but who are even more convinced and devout bearers of our worldview."* (Der Reichsführer-ᛋᛋ [8]   A bourgeois army which allows itself the luxury of a confusion of worldviews can never offer the necessary resistance to the Bolshevik army.

2. The soldierly virtues of loyalty, obedience and bravery cannot be fully developed if they are not based on the deep foundation of a unified worldview. A person's attitude is the result of his worldview. In Adolf Hitler's army and in the units of the peoples allied with the Reich, leader and man must represent the European cause with all consistency, not only in an intellectual but also in a conscious way. A people without a worldview or confused about the world will never be able to fight its way through to the final conclusions in the face of Bolshevism's consistently trained army, even if they otherwise possess inherent soldierly virtues.

3. This is why leaders and men in this struggle must be passionate advocates of the belief in the Führer as the trustee of the European conscience and in the Germanic Reich as the centre of a new order of Europe based on the community of the Folk. We must always be aware that in this war the enemy is trying to undermine the ideological stability of our people not only with his weapons but with all means of propaganda, by leaflets, radio and agents. The agitation and lying propaganda of the enemy, the political soldier alone is able to defend himself. Weapons alone will not help here.   Only the ideologically and passionately committed to the Führer and to National Socialism can stand up and win in this long and hard struggle. For all the peoples of Europe, however, the word that Dietrich Eckart

called out to his fatherland Germany at the time of the terror of the Bolshevik Jewish chieftain Béla Kun in Hungary applies:

"Woe to the nation that is still sleeping. Germany awake!"

Reference :

1) Adolf Hitler in his order to the army of 8. 1. 44.

2) "The way to the Reich", p. 45 ff.

3) "The Path of the NSDAP.", p. 6 ff.

4) "Americanism - A world danger", pp. 15 ff, 24 ff, 37 ff.

5) "Europe and Bolshevism", pp. 3-6.

6) "Political Education in the Red Army".

7) The Reichsführer-ϟϟ in his order of 24. 2. 43.

8) ϟϟ-Leitheft 1/43, 9. Jg., "Dein Soldatentum ist Weltanschauung".

Lesson 21

The National Socialist Worldview is an obligation for future generations

"See to it that the strength of our people receives its foundations not in colonies but in the soil of our homeland in Europe! Never think of the Reich as secure if it is not able to give every part of our people its own piece of land for centuries to come. Never forget that the most sacred right in this world is the right to the earth which one wants to cultivate oneself, and the most sacred sacrifice is the blood which one sheds for this earth."

Adolf Hitler: "Mein Kampf", p. 754

I. Our historical heritage

The National Socialist Revolution has often been accused of breaking with all tradition and all the eternal values of the German people, and of trying to "make history" itself. It is in the nature of every genuine revolution that it first concludes the previous development once and for all. No revolution, however, can in the long run completely disregard the historical tradition. The National Socialist revolution has never been without tradition. It consciously harkens back to the high times of German history, and it first fulfils the longing of the greatest of the people. When National Socialism coined the concept of the Third Reich, it consciously inserted itself into the historical process of development of the German people. The historical uniqueness of National Socialism's work

The historical uniqueness of National Socialist activity already allows us to recognise several major stages. From National Socialist Germany became the Greater German Reich, and in the present war this Reich itself became the Reich par excellence, the first organising power in Europe and the guarantor of its security. On the way to the Reich, National Socialism has always been deeply aware of its historical mission. In his great cultural speeches at the Reich Party Rallies, the Führer has always professed anew the immortal works of German masters. What would the idea of a Reich be without a world-historical past!

Today we feel just as committed to the spirit of the German cathedral builders as we do to the defiant faith of Luther's confession: "Even if the world were full of devils, we must succeed. Our time affirms in the same way the internalised faithfulness of Bach's music or the shattering elemental power of Beethoven's symphonies as it does the nobility of Prussian style in the Frederician age. It is the same attitude that binds us to everything. If, however, we are able today to deeply understand and relive the creations and experiences of the most important German life, then it is our most sacred certainty that with the Reich created through blood, the Reich in our hearts will also grow.

II. Obligations from two world wars

Under the shattering impression of the German collapse, still in hospital, the Führer decided to become a politician. If it was the fervent will to help his people rise again that moved him to this decision, it was no less his obligation to the two million who had fallen that made him do so. In view of the betrayal and the November Revolution, the Führer asks: *"Did the German soldiers go hungry, thirsty and freezing, tired from sleepless nights and endless marches? Had he lain for it in the hell of the drum fire and in the fever of the battle, without which, ever mindful of the one and only task of protecting his Fatherland from the invasion of the enemy? Truly, these heroes also deserved a stone: Wanderer, you who come to Germany, tell your homeland that we lie here, loyal to the fatherland and obedient to our duty"*. ("Mein Kampf", p. 224).

In all his struggle for the people, the Führer has always been conscious of the sacrifice of those who died in the World War as a reminder of his duty. And when, on 1 September 1939, he once again put on the uniform which he confessed *"was once the holiest and most precious"* to him, he assured the world that 9 November 1918 will never be repeated for a second time in German history. And this is our responsibility: it must not happen again! The army of the dead from the two greatest wars in the world, which were fought for the survival of our nation and our Reich, commands this as the holiest appeal!

III. The "succession" of the future -the National Socialist Führer Principle

When the Führer put on the grey jacket on 1 September 1939 and thus placed himself under the law of war, he also laid down the form of succession to the Führer in the event that something should happen to him. He determined that in future the leader of the Reich should always be the most worthy, i.e., the bravest. This is a guarantee that only the best son of the people is also its leader. There will no longer be a monarchical succession, but performance and succession will make it possible to ascend to the highest ranks that the people and the nation have to offer. Because National Socialism watches over this genuine aristocracy of achievement and will guard and nurture it for the good of the people, it means an obligation for all future generations, since only through it will they be guaranteed an existence in freedom and dignity.

According to the will of the Führer, the systematic selection of capable people takes place in the educational institutions created by National Socialism. The Hitler Youth and the BDM are the great organisations which carry out a careful pre-selection. They see to it that the best people are brought to the National Socialist educational institutions and the Adolf Hitler schools. Every boy and girl then goes through the military service, the great "school of the nation", in order to become an armed force in the best sense of the word. Military service, however, will remain the crowning glory of manhood education for all time to come, and it will produce an arms-bearer who will guarantee the security of the Reich at all times.

SA, ⚡⚡ and the other branches of the party must ensure that an uncompromising, ideological militancy is constantly educated, then it is the task of the party's Order Castles to prepare the best from this militancy for future leadership tasks.

"A world-view which, while rejecting the democratic idea of the masses, endeavours to give this earth to the best people, i.e. to the highest human beings, must logically also obey the same aristocratic principle within this people and secure for the best minds the leadership and the highest influence in the people concerned. Thus it builds not on the idea of majority but on that of personality."

Adolf Hitler : "Mein Kampf", p. 493

IV. The Necessity of a Community of Wills

National Socialism as a mere world-view would be practically worthless if it were not the fanatical avowal of a community of wills determined to do everything. The Führer said:

"Worldview and national discipline meet on one level. Spiritual guidance and political leadership of the nation find their affirmation in the political will."

The Führer at the 1937 Reich Party Congress.

The bearer of this will shall be the political soldier as formed by National Socialism. Beyond this, however, a community is necessary which is able to use the concentrated power of an indomitable will in every hour. Great historical events are always brought about by outstanding personalities and by a will that is transmitted to their communities. Political and religious movements bear witness to what concentrated will can do. If a people are not possessed of a fanatical will of supremacy until the last decisive hour, no force, no matter how strong, can secure for it the freedom of existence and its future.

"Once this war is over, the greatest laurels will be due more to our faith and perseverance than to unique drive and thus individual actions."

Adolf Hitler

V. Guardian of the life of future generations

In his political testament, the Führer pointed out the necessity of securing the life of the nation by providing it with an adequate living space. The Reich will only be secure in the future if it can give each member his own piece of ground. Today the Reich and Europe are fighting for this living space, which is tantamount to being or not being for the future. According to the Führer's will, he is the first fighter for the new living space. He, who first realised the National Socialist doctrine of the racial idea through racial selection, is at the same time the most appointed guardian of the life of our descendants. For it is our belief that the chain of generations will not end with us.

"Thus we have set out and are marching according to unalterable laws as a National Socialist soldierly order of Nordic men and as a sworn community of their clans along the path into a distant future, wishing and believing that we would like to be not only the grandchildren who fought it out better, but beyond that the ancestors of the latest generations necessary for the eternal life of the Germanic people."

Heinrich Himmler

SS
HANDBLÄTTER
FÜR DEN WELTANSCHAULICHEN UNTERRICHT

Lesson 22

This is the way of the SS

"Any description of the organisation, task and structure of the SS cannot be understood if one does not try to grasp it inwardly with one's blood and heart".

Heinrich Himmler

Whoever wears the runes of the SS and fights in the ranks of the Waffen-SS must also know about the development of the SS. As a branch of the National Socialist movement, its development is closely linked to the Führer's struggle for the renewal of the German people. This struggle has shaped their nature.

I. The Schutzstaffel

From the smallest beginnings (1923 "Stabswache" and "Stoßtrupp Hitler", 1925 the "Zehner schaften") the Schutzstaffel emerged.

Their task:

a) Protecting the Führer at rallies and propaganda drives, if necessary at the risk of his own life (comparison: SA. - hall protection);

b) Guarantor of the party's internal security (comparison: police, state security).

Prerequisites for the fulfilment of these tasks: unconditional loyalty to the Führer, total commitment of the person, iron discipline. It was not the number of men that was decisive, but their ideological and soldierly qualities.

Soon the propagation of the idea was added as a new task (through discussion, leaflets, party press, "Mein Kampf"). Thus, the political soldiering of the party began to emerge at an early stage.

At the Reich Party Congress in Weimar in 1926, the Führer hands over the blood flag of 9th November 1923 to the protection of the ⚡⚡.

At the beginning of January 1929, there are 270 ⚡⚡-men throughout Germany.

On 6th January 1929 Heinrich Himmler takes over the leadership of the ⚡⚡. This marks the beginning of the decisive development: the expansion of the ⚡⚡ as the elite formation of the party, the eternally vigilant guardian of the Reich.

II. The four main virtues

In order to lead such tasks to full success, the ⚡⚡ had from the outset adopted the principle of selection. The following four main virtues are the principles on which this selection was based:

1. Purity of Blood:

Affirmation of racial laws. Selection of the Nordic-determined man (later renewed selection according to performance and probation).

From the order to men of the clan community, stated in the Engagement and Marriage Order of the Reichsführer-⚡⚡ (31st December, 1931), which elevates marriage and race to basic principles of the clan community.

The strength of a people is not determined by the value of its hereditary property alone; in the struggle for living space and the right to live, the fertility of a people and the number of its children are decisive.

This is why the *"victory of the child"*, which provides for the offspring of fallen comrades, and also includes the precious children of natural birth

2. The will for freedom and fighting spirit:

Unconditional upholding of all soldierly virtues. Steeling of the body. Always on guard!

"Much rather fight and die honestly than lose freedom and corrupt soul."

Banner slogan of Strasbourg

"There will always be a group of really active fighters, and the nation demands more of them than the millions. To say "I believe" is not enough for them. They must swear " I FIGHT!"

Adolf Hitler, Party congress 10th September 1934

The constant willingness to fight is achieved through sporting achievement in annual performance examinations and through sensible world-view training.

3. Loyalty and Honour:

The worst offence is disloyalty. This means disloyalty to the ancestors and their laws, as well as disloyalty to comrades, and disloyalty to the leader as well as to oneself. The Führer's motto for the : " ᛋᛋ-Mann, deine Ehre heißt Treue!"

"The mind may stumble, that is sometimes harmful, but never incorrigible. But the heart has always the same pulse to beat, and if it ceases, the man dies just as his people die if they break fidelity. By this we mean loyalty of any kind, loyalty to the Führer and thus to the Germanic people, their knowledge and their kind, loyalty to the blood, to our ancestors and grandchildren, loyalty to our clan, loyalty to our comrade and loyalty to the immutable laws of decency, cleanliness and chivalry".

Heinrich Himmler

The order on the sanctity of property, equating the cigarette with the greatest preciousness. There is a deep meaning in the fact that no locked cupboards are allowed in the barracks of the ᛋᛋ

4. Discipline:

Bravery and courage on the one hand, unconditional obedience on the other. Obedience in the ᛋᛋ is a voluntary obedience.

Always remaining master of one's own life, that is what makes the ᛋᛋ-man master even over the political and military opponent.

"It does not depend on how many glasses of beer he is able to drink, but only on how many blows he can endure, not on how many nights he is able to stroll through, but on how many kilometres he can march."

Adolf Hitler

Discipline of body and soul is the prerequisite for all performance!

III. Fighters for the National Socialist Worldview

On the day of the seizure of power (30 January 1933), the ᛋᛋ had grown to 51,000 men: a self-sustaining force, dedicated to the Führer's life and death.

In a necessary continuation of the development, the task of monitoring the internal security of the Party is now joined by the task of securing the internal security of the state. Heinrich Himmler becomes head of the German police (17 June 1936).

Today's tasks of the ᛋᛋ and police: To enforce the will of the state, guarantor of public order desired by the state; safeguarding the German people as an organic whole, its vitality and its institutions against destruction and decomposition.

Behind these tasks, however, is the ultimate goal: to create, through education and selection, a new type of man - and leader - who is capable of mastering all the great tasks of the future: the political soldier.

A fighter for our worldview, for our faith.

Not only as a party comrade, but also as a soldier, the ᛋᛋ-man has a very special relationship to politics. He is the continuator, the fighter and the moral finisher with his powers and means, thanks to the sacrifice of his blood.

Yesterday, politics was the plaything of the parties and the powers; National Socialism created a unified Reich politic.

This has also put the soldier and his struggle on a secure footing. He must be a messenger and a fighter for a Germanic-German way of being, he must use both idea and weapon with equal strength.

The new type of this consciously "political" soldier has found its most visible expression in the Waffen-ᛋᛋ

Reference :

Heinrich Himmler: "The Schutzstaffel as anti-Bolshevik fighting organisation".

SS

HANDBLÄTTER
FÜR DEN WELTANSCHAULICHEN UNTERRICHT

Lesson 23

The SS, Stormtroops of the new Europe

I. The Waffen-SS

The beginnings of the Waffen-SS go back to the spring of 1933. In the course of the security measures, the Führer ordered the formation of the first active barracked formation of the SS: the "Leibstandarte Adolf Hitler".

Within the framework of the further expansion of the SS-Verfügungstruppen, the establishment of the SS-Standarten "Deutschland" in Munich and "Germania" in Hamburg.

The first deployment of the Waffen-SS took place in connection with the homeland of the Eastern March and the Sudetenland. The SS-Standarte "Der Führer" was established in the Danube meadows. The further expansion of the Waffen-SS went hand in hand with the development of the political situation: the creation of the Protectorate, the fight in and around Danzig, the Polish campaign brought new inputs; new forces emerged, and the standards grew into Divisions.

If the SS clearly and unequivocally demanded a rebirth of Germanism from the outset, it was also called upon to address the entire Germanic people beyond the former borders and to promote the Germanic idea. By setting up SS units in the Germanic countries, vanguards were won for a future development.

After the victorious conclusion of the Norwegian and French campaigns, the Waffen-SS took on their mission on a broader basis. From Norway, Denmark, Holland, Flanders came the influx of volunteers into the SS-Standarten "Nordland" and "Westland" in 1941.

"Germany has not only asked us, we ourselves feel obliged. We now want to do everything we can of our own free will to fight at Hitler's and Germany's side for the Germanic Volksgemeinschaft and the new Europe."

Quisling , the leader of the Norwegian Nationalists

The campaigns in the Balkans and against the Bolsheviks were followed by the rise of the national Romanian, Croatian, Latvian, Estonian, and Hungarian SS formations.

Thus, men from all European countries fought and still fight shoulder to shoulder in the ranks of the Waffen-SS against Bolshevism and its Jewish backers.

II. From the Germanic to the European Task

In its course of more than four years, the war has shown the German people ever wider horizons of its future task. Today, whether it likes it or not, Germany is faced with the question of the future of the European continent. Only the completion of German unity has given Germany the strength to carry out this task.

The solution to this task does not only consist in a war with weapons. The problem of the new co-existence of the European peoples must be solved in its entire historical and present scope. The more and more lost awareness of the global community has been re-awakened and has found expression in the Dutch, Danish and Norwegian Waffen-SS formations.

This war is an ideological war. Just as the state conceptions of the past had to give way to the idea of the Reich, so today the common Germanic idea fits in with the multifaceted problem of peoples on the European continent.

Here, however, Germany occupies its special place, which is conditioned by its fateful development, its historical responsibility and the gravity of its blood sacrifices.

Hence the self-evidence of leadership, hence the fact that the European peoples are seeking to align themselves with Germany, hence the establishment of the various European formations of the Waffen-SS.

"Germany is called to liberate all the cultivated peoples of the mainland, not by seeking to impose its peculiarity on foreign peoples, but by pointing each people to itself and its particular history."

Henrik Steffens

II. The Waffen-SS Stormtroop of the European task

The Waffen-SS as the embodiment of political soldiering - stand as a shock troop in the military and political field.

The feats of arms of the SS formations attach indelible honour and immortal glory to their banners. The repeated mention of SS formations in the Wehrmacht report obliges the highest soldierly efforts and achievements.

The harshness of the political situation is not as visible to the public, but these political problems do not weigh any lighter.

They begin with the personal attitude of the individual ᛋᛋ-man: he must be honest, obedient, faithful and open; his conviction must be communicated to those around him (family, clan, people); he is a supporter of the greatest political idea of the century.

If he himself is regarded with respect by others, his word will carry more weight; if his way of life is the true expression of his worldview, he will easily convince others.

What is true for the individual is also true for all. The ideological attitude of the Waffen-ᛋᛋ is their most important political tool. The attitude they exemplify is their best weapon in the ideological-political struggle. The greater the extent of this struggle, the more comprehensive, responsible and hard it will be. The Waffen-ᛋᛋ stands in this soldierly and ideological struggle in complete dedication and unchanging loyalty.

Once the ground is prepared in this way, all decisions become easy. The Waffen-ᛋᛋ as fighter and herald will use weapon and idea in the same way. Thus, the ground for the future is broken up with the sword and sown with the seed of the idea. The peasant and the craftsman, the girls and the women place their hope and their faith in the Waffen-ᛋᛋ as the pioneers of a new European future.

For America and Britain Europe is only a colony, for the Jews and Bolsheviks only an object for exploitation - for the European peoples Europe is the heart of the world. If the heart stops beating, the body dies. Therefore, those who fight in the ranks of the Waffen-ᛋᛋ must know why they are defending their homeland against the onslaught of a worldview that is alien to Europe in terms of race and nature, and that they are fighting for the re-organisation of Europe. This New Order will be a common order, within which each member will take its place and rank according to performance and commitment for the whole and on the basis of the particularity and peculiarity of the individual people.

Therefore, those who fight in the ranks of the Waffen-ᛋᛋ must know why they are defending their homeland against the onslaught of a worldview that is alien to Europe in terms of race and nature, and that they are fighting for the re-organisation of Europe. This new order will be a common order, within which each member will take its place and rank according to performance and commitment for the whole and on the basis of the particularity and peculiarity of the individual people.

Thus, it is in the power of each individual ᛋᛋ-man to contribute to the final decision through his personal commitment, thus the ᛋᛋ has grown from the German to the Greater German, from the Greater German to the Germanic, from the Germanic to the European task as a

Stormtrooper for a new Europe.

"Only brave peoples have a secure existence, a future, a development; weak peoples perish, and that is correct."

Heinrich v Treischke

"May every single German, no matter where he stands, be aware that on himself, on his commitment and willingness to sacrifice, depends the preservation of our people, the fate and future of many generations."

Adolf Hitler on 10 September 1943

Reference:

Heinrich Himmler: "The Schutzstaffel as anti-Bolshevik fighting organisation".

Lesson 24

Our goal – a strong and united Europe

Outline:

I. What does the Reich mean for Europe?

II.   What political idea does the Reich bring to the new Europe?

III.   How should the peoples of Europe live together?

IV. What is our goal?

I.   What does the Reich mean for Europe?

Europe is fighting for its existence.

From the East the armies of the communist world revolution threaten. They bring absolute annihilation.

From the Atlantic threatens the invasion of the Jewish vultures of prey from New York. Every day and every night they send us their terror bombers. They seek the destruction and plundering of Europe.

In this enormous war on two fronts, it is necessary to gather all European forces.[1]

Only our own strength can save Europe. The alert peoples of Europe have rallied around the Reich in the fight against Bolshevism and Americanism. It is in this struggle, above all in the Waffen-SS, that the community of the new Europe is born.

Germany is the heartland of Europe, the Reich the strongest military power in the continent.

Therefore, the Reich must assume the military leadership of the continent. No other European nation could take its place. The Reich is the leading European power.

II. What political idea does the Reich bring to the new Europe?

107

In 6 short years of peace, Adolf Hitler has led the German people out of disorder and turmoil and into order, out of misery and hardship and into secure bread. Overcame unemployment and thus restored life to its full meaning.

He overcame Germany's weakness and powerlessness as a state, developed our economic strength and restored our respect and standing in the eyes of the world. The Führer has restored German honour.

He has eliminated the poison of Jewish decomposition in

Trade and Commerce,

Theatre and Entertainment,

Art and Science.

purified these areas of life and led them towards new prosperity. He successfully fought against the uprooting and endangerment of the German people and initiated a revival of the German nation. Recalling the eternal laws of life, he founded the measures for the preservation and development of a viable racial foundation of the people. He restored our relationship with the soil. He awakened in us faith in our future and with it the desire to have children. He gave us back the joy of happy life.

The Führer overcame the idea of class struggle from above as well as from below and founded the national order as a union of all Germans in one Reich and as an internal order in a true people's cooperative. This national order gives everyone the opportunity to fully develop their strengths. The most able can and should come to the top.

The Führer says:

"We are facing a state in which in the future every position will be occupied by the most capable son of our people, regardless of where he comes from; a system in which birth is nothing and achievement and ability are everything".

All of these aspirations and ideas are summed up in the concept of National Socialism. Its principles are

a) Achievement,

b) Property, which obliges to perform for the national community,

c) Protection of labour,

d) Honour of labour,

e) Freedom of personal development in creative achievement.

Under the sign of this folkish socialism, the whole people become a great community.

In such a community, the individual can fully develop his or her social abilities in service to the whole people. In a life without oppressive hardship and fear, in a life of order and peace, the artistic creative forces develop into mature achievements of lasting value.

This solution of the social question in the spirit of a National Socialism has given the Reich, in a few years, an undreamed-of development and blossoming.

Every nation in Europe is faced with the task of solving the social problem.

Capitalism has caused the social question, but according to its principle of profit-seeking and crass egoism, it can never eliminate social needs in a just solution. It can give alms, but will never establish the right of the worker.

Bolshevism cannot solve the social question because its Jewish originators do not think of the welfare of the peoples, but only of their own power.

Therefore, Bolshevism brought only fear, misery and exploitation to the peoples of the East.

Only Folkish socialism can solve the social problem, because it wants the happiness of the people. The Führer himself is proud to be a formerly unknown son and soldier of this people, he knows its needs and wants nothing other than a *"social state of the highest culture"*.

The political idea which the Reich gives to the new Europe is the idea of folk socialism.[2]

III. How do the peoples of Europe want to live together ?

The Reich is the natural rallying point and centre of Europe, the German people a member of the European racial community.

The relationship of the Reich to Europe is not the form of imperialism subjugating the people. The imperialist state does not know the concept of people and race and therefore cannot respect them.

In imperialist states, minorities are brutally oppressed or forced to change their nationality (Polonisation, Czechisation, Russification, Hungarianisation).

The European family of nations, on the other hand, will be a family of peoples. Its members stand in the same relationship to each other as the Volksgenossen in the Volksgemeinschaft of the Reich. Above this family of peoples stands the principle: European common good comes before national self-interest.

Each member of this family of peoples is rooted in its own nationality and can only make the best contribution to the cultural life of Europe as a whole by preserving and developing its own racial-ethnic characteristics in a manner appropriate to its life. There will therefore be no "conformity" and impoverishing uniformity. Each nation will make its own individual contribution out of genuine racial and ethnic identity.[3]

Europe has given much to the world. The great achievements of civilisation and culture of the world are overwhelmingly of European origin. Americanism and Bolshevism only draw on what Europe has given them.

European culture will be the force that will secure Europe's place on earth and the development of its living space in the future.

IV. What is our goal?

To secure for the German people a life in freedom and honour and to see them as members of a happy European family of nations. The peoples of Europe should no longer weaken each other through fratricidal wars, but should use all their powers in free development to achieve a greater overall achievement. A new age of order and construction will see Europe as the leading cultural power on earth, finding its highest happiness in creative achievement.

Reference :

Training Papers of the ϟϟ-Hauptamt

1) Europe and Bolshevism, p. 3.

2) Europe and Bolshevism, pp. 6f.

3) The Reich and Europe, p. 48, last paragraph.

SS HANDBLÄTTER

FÜR DEN WELTANSCHAULICHEN UNTERRICHT

Lesson 25

Our strongest weapon - our fanatical belief in victory

"The strength of men is not shown in the evening after victory, but when the sun once does not shine. The brave man will take up the fight anew in fierce defiance."

Adolf Hitler

In addition to our military strength and the united labour power of the peoples of Europe, we have as our strongest weapon to oppose the will of the enemy to annihilation our faith in the mission of Adolf Hitler and in the National Socialist idea.

I. The Power of Faith in History

What a nation is worth, it proves in the hours of probation. In the greatest adversity it puts to the test the purity of faith in its good cause.

1.The Great Prussian King is a unique historical example of the power of faith and will even after severe setbacks. After the defeat of Kolin in 1757, the nimbus of invincibility had been taken from the Prussian army, and an overpowering coalition of enemies was given time to develop against little Prussia. The King, however, wrote: *"In such hopeless times, one must provide oneself with iron guts and a brazen heart in order to become devoid of all sensitivity."* The steadfastness of the King and his army helped Prussia through this difficult hour. The fate of the small Prussian state literally hung by a thread until the last year of the Seven Years' War. The King was only able to keep his head above water by lightning-fast operations, sometimes in the west, sometimes in the south and south-east. But the King suffered his most serious defeat on 12 August 1759 at Kunersdorf. The downfall of the Fatherland seemed certain. *"I will not survive the downfall of my Fatherland,"* the King wrote. What saved Prussia in the last hour was the King's brazen heart. *"The officers and I are determined to die or to conquer, heaven willing that the common soldier should think likewise."* And only two days after the catastrophe, the King took over the supreme command again and mastered fate.[1]

2. The Führer's life is an equally wonderful example of the power of faith in one's own cause to move mountains.

Here are just a few dates:

In 1918, the year of the collapse, the Führer lay blinded by gas in the military hospital in Pasewalk. He buried his head in the pillows, crying, when he received the news of the collapse of the Fatherland and decided to turn his fate around and become a politician.

On 9 November 1923, the hope of a resurrection of the Reich from the shackles of the Versailles Dictate collapsed once again. But the dead of the Feldherrnhalle are the seeds of resurrection. During his one-year incarceration in Landsberg, the Führer writes his book "Mein Kampf" (My Struggle) and, after his release from prison, starts all over again. Through countless setbacks, through terror, imprisonment of his loyal followers, bans on speech, street battles, through the flood of hatred from the entire press and public opinion, through contempt and personal hardship, he sticks steadfastly to his belief in the resurrection of his people until the glorious day of 30 January 1933 [2]

The historical development of the Führer and his movement is an example of the power of faith in the life of the people. He achieves the miracle of the breakthrough of a minority over a superior majority, which has all external means of power at its disposal. Only a nation that struggles through difficult adversity can win the fate and the all-embracing victory that master's fate and brings it about.

What is true for the life of the Führer is true for the German people and the peoples of Europe who are struggling for their liberation from the poison of Jewish and Masonic alienation.

II. Our faith - the secret of our strength

We believe in the will of Providence which plunged our nation, as the first nation in Europe, into the deepest abyss and sent it through the misery of millions of unemployed, through years of shame and dishonour as a result of the Versailles Dictate and the thousandfold disenfranchisement of all Germans in the world into an unspeakably difficult school of life. In this school, our people gained the hardness, toughness and strength that enable them to endure what no people on this earth would endure in the same way.

We believe in the same Providence which at the last hour sent us the Führer who set the example of the purest sacrifice to his people and thus gained the power over their hearts which enabled him to become not only the liberator of Germany but also the liberator of all European peoples from the threat of the Steppe and the Jewish infiltration.

We believe that the dead Germans who have fallen on all the battlefields of Europe and lie far over in the East under the foreign soil have not fallen in vain. Their faith is our duty never to waver, no matter what comes.

We believe in the sovereignty of our nation in this world. If it were not for Germany, the world would be irreplaceably poorer. If the heart of Europe is torn from the centre of this continent, what remains is chaos and confusion.

We believe that the hour has come when the peoples of Europe have to prove by deed the commitment to their common standard of life and to the greatness of their common culture. The fertilising force that created the great cathedrals as the stone form of the dream and longing of our people, that gave rise to the masterpieces of music, painting and sculpture, that founded the Reich of the Kaisers, lives on in Adolf Hitler, the shaper of the new Germanic Reich, and is stronger than the law of numbers and all the huckster's souls in the cultureless plutocracies.

We believe in the education of Europe towards the countries of the Steppes, which have not produced a culture of their own and have erected a sinister system of terror over their own people with the ideas of Marxism, which they are prepared to spread over Europe and thus shroud our time-honoured continent in darkness.

The Reichsführer-ᛋᛋ spoke the following words in The Hague on the occasion of the swearing-in of the Dutch ᛋᛋ to the Führer:

"For millennia our peoples of Germanic blood have been pursuing their path of great history, but this never led to the really great result, to the great homeland of all Germanic blood. After thousands of years of the greatest hardship, when sub-humanity set in, after a world war to attack the states of Europe, fate gave us all the Führer, and in this time, my men, we are allowed to live in this time we have the opportunity to show what we are worth, what our ancestors are worth, and what our grandchildren will be worth."

Our faith in the Führer and the Germanic Reich is stronger than all the threats, it grows with the measure of hardship and will compel fate.

"Cowardly thoughts, timid swaying, womanly lamenting, fearful trembling

Will not turn away misery, will not set you free.

To all powers, to keep yourself safe, Never bow down,

Show yourself strong. Summon the arms of the gods!"

Goethe

Reference :

1) -Leitheft 3/44, 10. Jahrgang, "Kunersdorf".

2) Lehrplan f. d. weltansch. Erziehung in der ᛋᛋ und Polizei, p. 57 ff.

Before Julian Assange and Edward Snowden astonished the world with their revelations about US secret documents, the Canadian James Bacque published his book "Other Losses" as early as 1989. The foreword was written by the US military historian Colonel Dr. Ernest F. Fisher.It is a detailed examination of how the US Army and the French Army became guilty of the deaths of about one million German prisoners of war - on the highest orders, but unnoticed by the world public. Together with the US army historian, Bacque analysed numerous American documents. They were able to prove that immediately after the German surrender, General Dwight Eisenhower, later President of the United States, had given the order to deny weather protection and food to the millions of German soldiers and civilian prisoners fenced in under the open sky. The Morgenthau Plan for the "pastoralisation" of Germany had been drafted by Roosevelt and Churchill at a secret conference in 1944. It envisaged the starvation of millions of prisoners of war and civilians - including Germans expelled from the East. Under the guise of "reparations", industrial production sites were looted and everything still usable was taken away. Probably the biggest patent theft of all time took place - especially through the kidnapping of German specialists and highly trained professionals. It was not until 1946 that the situation for the maltreated people improved somewhat as a result of an extraordinary international relief action. It was led by the American Herbert Hoover ("Hoover Food") and the Canadian MacKenzie. Our documentary - based on a total of three books by Bacque - shows astonishing and harrowing new footage, supplemented by interviews with American commanders of the death camps and with German victims who survived these inhuman hardships.

Bevor Julian Assange und Edward Snowden mit ihren Enthüllungen über US-Geheimdokumente die Welt in Erstaunen versetzten, veröffentlichte der Kanadier James Bacque bereits 1989 sein Buch „Other Losses". Das Vorwort schrieb der US-Militärhistoriker Oberst Dr. Ernest F. Fisher.Es ist eine detaillierte Aufarbeitung, wie die US-Armee und die französische Armee schuldig wurden am Tod von etwa einer Millionen deutscher Kriegsgefangener - auf höchsten Befehl, jedoch unbemerkt von der Weltöffentlichkeit. Gemeinsam mit dem Historiker der US-Armee wertete Bacque zahlreiche amerikanische Dokumente aus. So konnten sie nachweisen, daß unmittelbar nach der deutschen Kapitulation General Dwight Eisenhower, später Präsident der Vereinigten Staaten, den Befehl erteilt hatte, den unter freiem Himmel eingezäunten Millionen deutscher Soldaten und Zivilgefangenen Wetterschutz und Nahrung zu verweigern. Der Morgenthau-Plan für die "Pastoralisierung" Deutschlands (Pastoralisierung = Umwandlung in Weideland) war 1944 von Roosevelt und Churchill auf einer Geheimkonferenz entworfen worden. Er sah die Aushungerung von Millionen Kriegsgefangenen und Zivilisten vor - einschließlich der aus dem Osten vertriebenen Deutschen. Unter dem Deckmantel „Reparationen" wurden industrielle Erzeugungsstätten geplündert und alles noch Brauchbare abtransportiert. Es fand der wohl größte Patentraub aller Zeiten statt – insbesondere durch die Entführung deutscher Spezialisten und hoch ausgebildeter Fachkräfte. Erst 1946 hat sich durch eine außerordentliche, internationale Hilfsaktion die Lage für das geschundene Volk etwas gebessert. Sie wurde geleitet von dem Amerikaner Herbert Hoover („Hoover Food") und dem Kanadier MacKenzie. Unsere Dokumentation - basierend auf insgesamt drei Büchern von Bacque - zeigt erstaunliches und erschütterndes neues Bildmaterial, ergänzt durch Interviews mit amerikanischen Kommandanten der Todeslager und mit deutschen Opfern, die diese unmenschlichen Strapazen überlebt haben.

DEUTSCH/ENGLISCH TON   GERMAN/ENGLISH LANGUAGE

www.realhistorybooks.co.uk

The Face of the Fuhrer/Das Antlitz Des Fuhrers

This the RAREST of Heinrich Hoffman's photograph albums produced in the Third Reich.

Produced in 1939 it has 16 spectacular full page portrait photographs covering the period 1919-1939. These photographs are the most dramatic Hitler portraits that were available to Hoffman at the time and each is identified by the year it was taken and a caption, in English and German, explaining the circumstances of the portrait.

It has an introduction by the leader of the Hitler Youth, Reichs Jugendfuhrer Baldur von Schirach describing the importance of the book.

This new edition has a sympathetic English translation of the original text and using the latest technology the portraits have been colourised. These have been further enhanced by only colourising Hitler himself so that he stands out even more with the background remaining in the original black and white.

Dies ist das Seltenste von Heinrich Hoffmans Fotoalben, das im Dritten Reich produziert wurde.

Produziert im Jahr 1939 hat es 16 spektakuläre ganzseitige Porträtfotos, die den Zeitraum 1919-1939 abdecken. Diese Fotografien sind die dramatischsten Hitler-Porträts, die Hoffman zu der Zeit zur Verfügung standen. Jedes ist mit dem Jahr der Aufnahme und einer Bildunterschrift in Englisch und Deutsch versehen, die die Umstände des Porträts erklärt.

Es hat eine Einleitung des Führers der Hitlerjugend, Reichsjugendführer Baldur von Schirach, der die Bedeutung des Buches beschreibt.

Diese neue Ausgabe hat eine einfühlsame englische Übersetzung des Originaltextes und die Porträts wurden mit modernster Technik koloriert. Die Porträts wurden mit modernster Technik koloriert, wobei nur Hitler selbst koloriert wurde, so dass er sich noch mehr abhebt, während der Hintergrund im ursprünglichen Schwarz-Weiß gehalten ist.

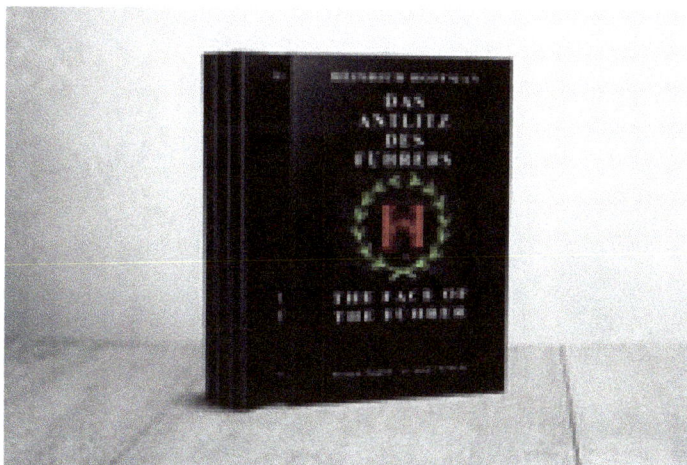

www.realhistorybooks.co.uk

New German Architecture /Neue Deutsche Baukunst

This is a dual language (German/English)reprint of the now extremely rare and expensive book, Neue Deutsche Baukunst, photobook published in 1941 and edited by Dr. Albert Speer to showcase the architectural beauty of the building programme instituted by National Socialist Germany. Book consists of photographs of these new structures with details of the architect or artist involved in the project. Even though it only existed for 12 years, and 6 of these were war years, the Third Reich left behind a rich heritage of buildings and statutes. With 96 pages this book highlights the most important new buildings of the Reich including the Nuremberg rally grounds, Military buildings and regional NSDAP headquarters.

Hitler's Revolution

Drawing on over 200 German sources, many pre-1945, Hitler's Revolution provides concise, penetrating insight into the National Socialist ideology and how it transformed German society. The government's success at relieving unemployment and its social programs to eliminate class barriers unlock the secret to Hitler's undeniable popularity which, in light of war crimes, seems so incomprehensible today.

Documents from German, Soviet and British archives help illuminate the diplomatic atmosphere of the times and the challenge Hitler confronted when weighing foreign policy decisions. Evidence shows that these were often spontaneous reaction to fluctuating political constellations rather than planned long in advance. During the war, oppressive German measures in occupied countries invited criticism from within Germany as the National Socialist dogma, particularly the race theory, began losing influence in official circles and the military.

An in-depth analysis of Hitler's wartime campaigns, especially Stalingrad and Normandy, reveals that the German resistance not only plotted to topple the regime, but systematically sabotaged combat operations causing the German army catastrophic defeats. The motive, historical records demonstrate, was not so idealistic as popularly believed. The author researched primarily German records, to present readers in the United States and Great Britain with information never before translated into English and otherwise inaccessible to them.

www.realhistorybooks.co.uk

Books – Translated from the Third Reich Originals!
Only a few of our many books are shown below.
Visit our web-site:

www.third-reich-posters.co.uk

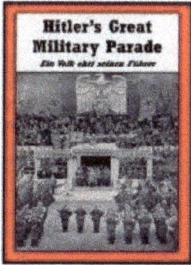

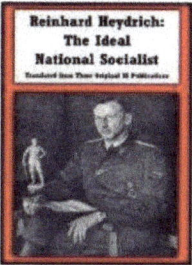

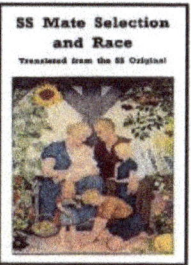

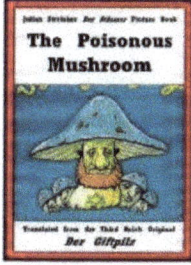

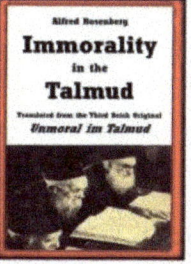

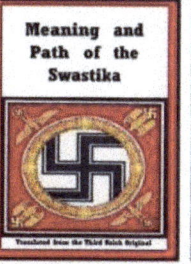

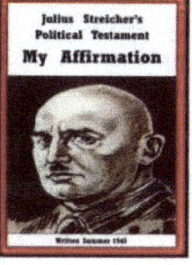

Adolf Hitler Speaks Volume One **The National Will**	Command and Obedience **SS Leadership Guide** FÜHRER BEFIEHL WIR FOLGEN!	**SS Defender against Bolshevism**	**SS Culture** Volume Eleven: **Beauty**	**The SS Calls You!**	**You and Your Folk**
The Reich Government	**Hitler's Great Military Parade**	**Reinhard Heydrich: The Ideal National Socialist**	**SS Mate Selection and Race**	**Bolshevism – Jewish Sub-Humanity**	**The Subhuman**
The Poisonous Mushroom	**Trust No Fox on Green Heath and No Jew on His Oath**	**SS Family Celebrations**	**The Eternal Jew** Volume One	**Hitler in Italy** HITLER in ITALIEN	**The Brown Army Das Braune Heer**
Luftwaffe War Art Die Luftwaffe im Bild	**Eternal Front**	**Discipline and Order**	**Immorality in the Talmud** Unmoral im Talmud	**Meaning and Path of the Swastika**	**Struggle for Berlin** Volume One: Fresh Start BERLIN!
Blood and Honor Volume One Against the Old System	**My Political Awakening**	Julius Streicher's Political Testament **My Affirmation**	Theodor Fritsch **The Sins of High Finance**	**The Party Program** Essence, Principles and Goals of the NSDAP	**Basic Ideas of National Socialist Cultural Policy**

117

www.ingramcontent.com/pod-product-compliance
Lightning Source LLC
Chambersburg PA
CBHW040802050426
42336CB00066B/3448